I Will Survive...
and You Will Too

I Will Survive...

and You Will Too

Tammy Faye Messner

Jeremy P. Tarcher / Penguin
a member of
Penguin Group (USA) Inc.

Most Tarcher/Penguin books are available at special quantity discounts for bulk purchase for sales promotions, premiums, fund-raising, and educational needs. Special books or book excerpts also can be created to fit specific needs. For details, write or telephone Penguin Group (USA) Inc. Special Markets, 375 Hudson Street, New York, NY 10014.

Jeremy P. Tarcher/Penguin
a member of
Penguin Group (USA) Inc.
375 Hudson Street
New York, NY 10014
www.penguin.com

Library of Congress Cataloging-in-Publication Data
Messner, Tammy Faye, date.
I will survive—and you can too / Tammy Faye Messner.
p.   cm.
ISBN 1-58542-242-8 (acid-free paper)
1. Messner, Tammy Faye, date.   2. Christian biography—United States.   I. Title.
BR1725.M43A3   2004   2003056522
277.3'082'092—dc22
[B]

Printed in the United States of America
1   3   5   7   9   10   8   6   4   2

This book is printed on acid-free paper. ∞

Book design by Lovedog Studio

I dedicate this book to my husband of ten years, Roe Messner. His quiet, peaceful nature and his unwavering faith in God inspire all who meet him, and the lessons he has taught me have enriched my life. He taught me that there *is* a life after tragedy. He has taught me how to live in peace, to be myself, and not to let anyone intimidate me. He has urged me on when I wanted to quit and has helped me build back a self-esteem that I thought was gone forever. The twinkle in his eyes keeps our marriage fun and fulfilling. We are not only lovers, we are best friends. We are comfortable together. He calls me "Monkey"; I won't tell you what I call him! Ha! Ha! He is the consummate gentleman who still opens the door for his wife.

Acknowledgments

There are some very special people in my life that I would like to take this opportunity to say thank you to.

First of all, my daughter, Tammy Sue Bakker, and my son, Jamie Charles Bakker. Thank you, kids, for always being there for Mom. I love you two; you are my heart. Thank you, Sissy, for having James and Jonathan and making me a grandma. And thank you, Jamie, for bringing your beautiful Amanda into our family.

My girlfriends have been a great source of love and encouragement to me over the years. I want them to know how important they are to me. Thank you: Deborah Lilly, Joyce Cordell, Judy Bycura, Gloria Weigand, Shirley Fulbright Martin, Sally Wall, Mona Lewis, Cheri Baldwin, Maryanna Yoxall, Rev. Sarah Utterbach, Zonell Thompson, Sharon Dygert, Jude Walker, Emma Howard, Mary Hutchinson, Fran Moore, Melony Hart, Sigrid Zenker, Cheryl Coleman, Bobbie Garn, Sandi Watson, and my cousin, Phyllis Tanner. And I cannot forget you, Patty Sewell. Patty died unexpectedly a few months ago. Patty, I miss you so much.

The women I have mentioned are "women of substance." They are godly women. They have been a part of my life for many years. I don't know what I would have done without them. I am proud to be able to call these wonderful women my friends. They say you are fortunate if you can count your close friends on one hand. God has blessed me beyond measure.

Last, but certainly not least, I want to thank the wonderful people who asked me to write this book. They put no demands on me as to content. They allowed me to write my heart. My thanks goes to my publisher, Joel Fotinos, my editor, Denise Silvestro, my publicist, Kelly Groves, and to John Strausbaugh, Amy Halliday, and Alan Stephenson.

Contents

IT'S A BUMPY RIDE, SO HANG ON!

GOD LOVES YOU JUST THE WAY YOU ARE—HE REALLY DOES

LESSONS WORTH LEARNING

Introduction

If you were to ask someone who knows me well, "What is Tammy Faye really like?" they would more than likely answer with, "What you see is what you get." And I guess that's me, all right. For years, people have tried to change me into what they think I should be. And for years I have fought to "just be me"; I don't know how to be someone else.

If you don't know me, I hope that through this book we will become friends. I sat at my old typewriter, Diet Coke in hand, for many months writing what is on these pages. I have written "my heart." I do think my very heart came through my fingers and landed on these pages.

I had *you* on my mind as I was writing. I wanted you to laugh, I wanted you to cry with me. But most of all, ally, I wanted to help you make it through the difficult times of your life.

As a little four-foot-eleven-inch girl from International Falls, Minnesota, my life has gone far beyond what I ever dreamed it could. Far beyond the happiness I dreamed, far beyond the sorrow I never dreamed of. But I'm still here, still laughing, still crying, still singing . . . And I give all the credit to One who

never left me, never forsook me, even in the hardest of times—
the Lord Jesus Christ.

To help you know me better, allow me to tell you about
my life:

1. My former husband, Jim Bakker, and I helped build the
   third largest Christian television network in the world—Pat
   Robertson's CBN. We worked with Pat for nine years. Next,
   we built the Trinity Broadcasting Network (TBN), now
   run by Paul Crouch. Finally, we built PTL-TV, the largest
   Christian television network in the world at that time. PTL
   was the third most visited place in the U.S. after Disneyland
   and Disney World.

2. I have been on TV for over half my life—thirty-five years.

3. I have recorded twenty-five albums, two of which went gold.

4. I have written five books, two of which were on the best-
   seller list.

5. For years I did my own TV show called *Tammy's House
   Party*.

6. I later did a secular television show with Jim J Bullock called
   The Jim J and Tammy Faye Show.

7. I have played Mimi's mom on *The Drew Carey Show*.

8. A documentary, *The Eyes of Tammy Faye*, was made about
   my life and won an award at the Sundance Film Festival.

But best of all, I am the mother of Tammy Sue Bakker and
Jamie Charles Bakker, and the grandmother of James and
Jonathan—Tammy Sue's children.

I have remarried. My husband's name is Roe Messner. He is the most gentle, kind, giving man I have ever met. Oh, and he's so handsome! He has brought a great quietness and peace to my life. He and I are exact opposites, which is good for me, at least! In October 2003 we will have been married ten years— and we're still on our honeymoon!

And I just lost twenty-five pounds!

My statistics: I am 4 feet 11 inches tall—at least that's my story, and I'm going to stick to it! My husband says I'm four feet ten and a half. Well, I tease my hair real high!

I weigh—oops!—a woman never tells her weight or her age.

My hair color is red . . . at least that's what it is today; I don't remember what color it used to be! But don't count on it staying this color. Next week I may go blond. They didn't know what color to put on my driver's license! They were so confused.

I wear a size 5–5½ shoe, which is so hard to find. I've always wished my feet were bigger. I wonder if it would have spoiled some great eternal plan if God would have made me five feet one inch with a size 7½ shoe. I'll just have to ask Him when I get to Heaven.

Well, I would just like to say, "Welcome to my world!"

Love always,
Tammy Faye

Family and Friends— Life's Most Precious Treasures

1.

Run Toward
the Roar

I learned very early on in life what fear was.
Little kids aren't supposed to be afraid. They are supposed to
be able to live unencumbered by the things that adults face.
They should be free to play and laugh and run. They should feel
protected from anything that could hurt them. They should
not have to feel afraid.

My mother and real dad were divorced when I was just three
years old. At that time there was me and my little brother
Donny. All I remember is that all of a sudden Daddy was gone,
and I never saw him again. I don't remember any feelings that
I must have had—fear being one of them, I am sure. My mom
married another wonderful man shortly after the divorce was
complete. His name was Fred Grover, and he was to become
the only Daddy I ever knew. I loved him with all my heart. He
was so kind and good to my brother and me.

Little children are supposed to be able to hug and kiss their
daddies; they're supposed to be able to climb up on his lap so

he can tell them stories. They're supposed to be able to hug his neck and say, "I love you, Daddy."

I never did any of those things as a little girl. I don't know why. I can't remember anyone telling me I couldn't. It was something inside me that said to me, This is not your real daddy, and you must always be a lady around him. Where did that come from? I've often wondered. I longed to crawl up on his lap. I longed to hug him. I longed to kiss his face, to say, "Daddy, I love you." I think I missed so much as a child because I was unable to do those things that "real kids" do.

After Mom remarried, it wasn't long before babies started to come. One every two years. I was a little girl who grew up fast—I had to. Mom needed help, and I loved babies. Before I knew it, Larry came along, then Judy, then Danny, then John-nie, and after him came Debbie and Ruth. There was never a dull moment in our household.

I remember helping Mom wash clothes. She would move that big old ringer washing machine into the kitchen from the porch, heat water on the stove to fill the machine, then put a big tub under the wringer filled with cold water for rinsing, and washing clothes for ten people would begin. It was a hard job on washday. I can remember the sound of the clothes going *slosh, slosh, slosh* in the machine, and all the soap bubbles and the steam. Then Mom would use a long stick, or what looked like a stick, and pull the clothes out one piece at a time and run them through the ringer into the big tub of cold water. She'd stir them around till the bubbles were gone, run them back through the ringer, and put them into the big clothes basket on the floor. When the basket was full, we would each grab an end and carry it out to the clothesline. I'd hand her the clothes and pins, and she would put them on the line to blow in the summer breeze until dry. Then we'd bring them in, and every day when I came home from school, as well as on Saturdays, I would iron. By the time I had finished all the ironing, the process would start all over again. I didn't mind ironing. I loved getting the wrinkles out of things and making them nice and flat and smooth.

We had a busy, busy household. There was always something to do, as the little kids played outdoors. Rain or snow or sunshine, it didn't matter. The show must go on! There was cooking and cleaning and doing dishes, stacks and stacks of dirty dishes, and dirty, greasy pots and pans. There was certainly no time for me to be a kid.

Then Mom and Dad started to fight all the time. They yelled and yelled at each other, and I knew what it was to be afraid. My dad never hit my mom; it was just the constant yelling. I would run into the bedroom and hide under the bed and cover my ears with my hands and hum a little tune so I could not hear what they were saying. I was so scared that Dad would leave Mom and that we'd be alone with no one to take care of us. I was so afraid that someone would come and separate all us kids, and we would never see each other again. I don't know where I heard that things like that could happen, but in my heart I knew it could. I'd beg Mom not to yell at Dad. She would start to cry. "It's okay Mom, it's going to be all right," my little voice would say. I'd hug her and try to make her feel happy again.

I cannot imagine how hard it was for my mom with eight of us kids, and me being her only help. She was a fantastic cook, she made cream puffs that were so light I'd dream of them flying away. My mom took such good care of us kids. She was so creative and fun.

2.

Stinky Feet, or How to Help Your Child Cope with Divorce

I wrote this story for my grandchildren when their parents got divorced. Maybe you know a child who could benefit from this story. If so, tear it out and pass it on. Or better yet, read it to them yourself. They'll appreciate the time with you.

———

A family is the most wonderful thing in the whole world. Our family lives in a house with three bedrooms, a big yellow kitchen, a den, where we have our television, a living room for special times, and a dining room we use only for Thanksgiving meals, Christmas meals, or a birthday party. Our house has two bathrooms and a garage for our car.

I love my bedroom. It's where I keep all my stuff and sleep at night. I feel safe in my bedroom. I can go to my bedroom when I want to be alone and shut out the whole world. I read books, I play with my toys, and my favorite teddy bear is always waiting for me in my bedroom. My bedroom is also where I keep my clothes.

Our house has a yard with trees and a swing. And my favorite thing of all is my dog Muffin and my cat Tinkerbell. Muffin is a pound puppy. We went to the animal shelter and picked him out special. We adopted him. He is not very big, and he follows me wherever I go. Sometimes he even sleeps on my bed in my bedroom. He is my best friend. Tinkerbell is a funny cat. She lives out in our yard. She brings things like dead mice and lays them at the front door of our house. She thinks she's bringing us a present. She chases birds and sometimes catches one. Mom says that's just what cats do.

I take good care of my pets. I make sure they always have food and water every day. I leave a bowl of water down all the time for my pets, and I never forget to fill it every day. My mom says that without water my pets will die. I brush my cat and dog, and I take my dog on a walk every day. I even give my dog a bath in the bathtub. He shakes water all over the place and gets me all wet. That makes me laugh.

I go to school Monday, Tuesday, Wednesday, Thursday, and Friday. I take a big yellow bus to school. I meet all my friends on the bus. I have to get up very early in the morning so that I'm not late for the bus. If I'm late, the bus leaves without me, and then Mom or Dad has to take me to school in the car, and

I don't think they like to do that too much. They tell me that it's very important in life to always be on time for everything we do. They say that's the reason we have clocks, so we won't be late for stuff. I have a clock in my room. It rings when I'm supposed to get out of bed, then Mom comes into my room and uses a word called "responsibility." We have to be responsible, she says. I guess that means that I have to not only go to school every day but I have to be on time.

I don't go to school on Saturday or Sunday. I get to sleep as long as I want to sleep on Saturday. But on Sunday I go to Sunday school and to church. But after that I get to play all day with my neighborhood friends and Muffin and Tinkerbell.

My daddy goes to work every day. My mommy works real hard too. She works at our house. She cleans the house, washes our clothes, shops for groceries, cooks our meals, and takes me to the dentist and the doctor when I am sick. She gets up with me in the night if I get scared. She takes me to the beauty shop to get my hair cut. She takes me anywhere I have to go. She is a busy Mom. She calls our car Mom's Taxi.

I know Mom and Daddy love me. But something scary is happening at our house. I hear them yelling and screaming at each other when Daddy comes home from work. They don't think I hear them, but I do. They stop when I walk into the room. Mom hugs me and says everything is all right. I see Mommy crying a lot, and sometimes Daddy leaves in the car and doesn't come back until after I am in bed.

Sometimes when I hear them fighting I get scared, and I run to my room and I hide under my bed with Muffin. I cover my ears, close my eyes real tight, and try not to cry. I don't like it when Daddy goes away in the car, and I feel sad when I see Mommy crying. I hug Mommy and tell her not to cry, that everything is going to be all right. She hugs me back real hard.

I hear the car. Yay, Daddy is home. He comes in the house. He doesn't talk to Mommy, but he picks me up, throws me in the air, catches me, and tells me he loves me more than anything. I like it when Daddy throws me up in the air and catches me. I like it when we play ball in the yard. I like it when Daddy pushes me in the swing. I like it when he takes me in the car, just me and him, and we go get a hamburger and ice cream. I know my daddy loves me.

One night I heard my mommy and daddy talking in their bedroom. They thought I was asleep, but their voices were really loud and I was listening real hard. They were talking about something called "divorce." I had never heard that word before, but I knew it was not a good word, because Mommy was crying real hard and Daddy was yelling real loud. They did not know I was listening. I don't think they know that kids hear almost everything, that kids know when something is going wrong in their family. Kids are really smart. But kids can pretend too. They can pretend that everything is all right, but in our hearts we are so scared. We think that if we are really good, if we do everything right, if we do our chores, get up on time, make sure we don't miss the bus, take good care of our pets, that Mommy and Daddy won't fight anymore. So we try extra hard. I will try extra hard to be very good.

When I am old I will still remember the day Mommy and Daddy sat me down in the living room, and I found out what the word "divorce" meant. They told me they both loved me very much. Then they said that Daddy would be moving out of the house to go and live somewhere else. That they were not going to be married anymore.

I didn't understand how that could happen. You were always supposed to have Mommy and Daddy together. How could they suddenly not be married anymore? What is going to happen to *me?* Will they make me go live with someone else too? Why was this awful thing happening to me? Could I still call Mommy "Mommy," and would Daddy still be my daddy? "Don't you love me?" I asked "If you love me you'll stay together."

I was so scared! I got up and ran into my bedroom. I called Muffin, and together we crawled under the bed where we knew we were safe. I covered my ears with my hands and closed my eyes really tight. "Muffin, you will never leave me, will you?" I asked my dog. Muffin laid his head close to mine. I thought he was lucky to be a dog and not a kid—a kid who was about to lose everything that felt safe. I started to cry and cry and cry. Muffin licked my tears, as if to say, Don't worry, everything will be all right.

A few weeks later Mommy and Daddy went to what they called a "court." It was a big, scary-looking building. There was a man in a robe sitting behind a big desk. He looked scary too. After a lot of talking, the man behind the desk—they called him a "judge"—decided that Mommy would get primary custody of Muffin and me, and that Daddy would have visiting rights. Daddy would pay Mommy money to help take care of me. I could go and see Daddy whenever I wanted to, but he would be in a different house in a different part of town.

That was the saddest day of my life. I was mad at Mommy, and I was mad at Daddy, and I was mad at that man they called the judge. I cried all the way home. I didn't want to talk to Mommy ever again. "You sent Daddy away," I cried. "I don't love you anymore. You sent my daddy away." She was crying, too, trying to explain to me that it was going to be better this way. I didn't believe her. The car pulled up in the driveway, and I ran into the house straight for my bedroom. Muffin, Muffin, where are you? Muffin came running, and together we crawled under the bed. I put my arm around my dog and cried tears of anger, hurt, and fear.

When I woke up it was morning, and I knew I'd miss the bus if I didn't hurry and get ready for school. I ran out of the house without even saying goodbye to Mommy. She was mean, and I hated her for taking my daddy away from me. I would never love her again, I thought. Never!

The bus ride was awful. I got off the bus and waited for everyone to go into school. Then I ran as fast as I could to a big tree in the school yard. No one was allowed to climb it, but that day I did. I climbed to the top and felt safe hidden in its leafy branches. I don't know how long I was up in the tree when suddenly I heard a voice calling my name. Come down here, you belong in school. It was the school security guard. He took me kicking and screaming and crying to the principal's office. "I hate school," I screamed. "I hate everybody and everything." I felt like my heart had a hole in it. I felt like I couldn't breathe. My stomach was sick. All of a sudden I didn't know where I belonged. I was never going home again. I would just run away. Muffin and me.

The principal was a lady and she was wise. She called in three kids. I didn't know who they were. Each one told me that their mommy and daddy were divorced, and that they would be my friend, and if I needed to talk or ask questions they would be there for me. I couldn't believe my ears. There were other kids like me. I wasn't alone. I wasn't the only one whose daddy had gone away.

When the kids went back to class the principal put her arm around me and asked me if she could get me something to eat from the lunchroom. That was the best pizza I ever ate. The principal didn't make me go to class. She let me sit in her office and draw pictures. I drew a line between Mommy and Daddy, and I drew tears on my face. The principal walked me to the bus that day and told me not to be afraid, that everything would be all right.

The bus pulled up to our house and Daddy's car was there. My heart jumped for joy. "Daddy's home, Daddy's home," I cried. Mommy and Daddy are back together again. I ran into the house and jumped into my daddy's arms. Don't ever leave again, please Daddy! A look of sadness passed over his face. "It's my weekend to have you," he said. "You're going to my house for the next couple of days."

I was happy about that. Mommy helped me pack a little suitcase with my toothpaste and toothbrush, my pajamas, and a set of clothes. Can I take Muffin? "Sure," Daddy said. Me and Muffin walked out and jumped into Daddy's car. I waved goodbye to Mommy. Will you be all right by yourself, Mommy? She smiled and said she would be fine, and for me to be good and mind Daddy, but I saw tears in her eyes.

On the way to Daddy's house he explained to me that it wasn't just his house, but it was my house too. He told me that I would have my very own room, and that I could hang posters on my walls and pick out my own bedspread, that I would have a closet for my clothes and a place to keep my toys. He explained to me that now I have two houses. Both of them were filled with love for me, oh yes, and for Muffin and Tinkerbell too.

We got to our new house and I ran and looked at my room.

I couldn't wait to go with Daddy to the store for my posters. That night Daddy and I sat on our couch and we watched sports. I think his TV only gets the sports channel. We took off our shoes, ordered pizza, and watched basketball, wrestling, and golf. Me and Daddy are "buds." We are going to have fun hanging out together. I didn't have to take a bath for two whole days, but I did have to brush my teeth. Daddy said I only get one set of teeth and they have to last a lifetime. We don't want to get cavities.

On Sunday Daddy and I went to Sunday school. He went into the big people's class; I went to the kids' class. It seemed that everyone knew about Mommy and Daddy's divorce. I found out that lots of kids in my Sunday school class have two houses. The teacher asked if anyone would like to pray, and one of the kids prayed that his parents would get back together again. Our teacher explained to us that sometimes, no matter how much mommies and daddies try, they just can't live together anymore. She said we should not be mad at them. She said that God loves Mommy and Daddy even if they are divorced, and that God loves me, too, and that He will help everything to be all right. I felt better when I left Sunday school.

Daddy took me home to get Muffin, and then Mommy was waiting for me with open arms. I ran up to her and hugged her and said, "Mommy, I love you." I told her about my other house, I told her that Tiger Woods won the golf game we watched. She laughed and told me to go upstairs and take a bath. I think she could smell my stinky feet right through my Sunday school tennis shoes. She knows that us guys really don't care too much about stuff like stinky feet.

That night Mommy let Muffin sleep with me on top of the bed. I don't need to be scared anymore. My mommy loves me, my daddy loves me, Muffin and Tinkerbell love me, and God loves me. That is a lot of love! And there are a lot of other kids just like me who have learned about the word "divorce." It's not such a scary word anymore. But it will always be a sad word. And that's okay, because everything is going to be all right.

A Child Asks, "What Did I Do Wrong?"
How to Survive Divorce

Children face so many issues when their parents divorce. Parents need to be honest with their children. Choose your details. Don't accuse each other, and let the kids know it's not their fault. They didn't do anything wrong!

Here are some of the things a child may struggle with when parents divorce. Be aware of these issues and talk to your child about them.

✳ My parents are always fighting.

✳ What does the word "divorce" mean?

✳ What will happen to me if Mommy and Daddy leave each other? Who will I be with? Will I still have my sister, my brother? Will I still have my toys, my room, my stuff?

✳ If I have to choose, whom do I choose? If I choose Mom, will Dad be mad? If I choose Dad, will Mom be mad? I'm scared! *(continued)*

A Child Asks, "What Did I Do Wrong?" *How to Survive Divorce (cont'd)*

✳ I don't want to move to a new place (probably smaller, a new neighborhood). I will miss my friends.

✳ If one parent moves out of state, do I have to fly to see them or get on a bus by myself? (You are never alone. God is always with you, and He will send your guardian angel to take care of you. We each have a guardian angel.)

✳ I don't like my new house or my new neighborhood! I hate Mom, I hate Dad! I hate everyone!

✳ I refuse to understand—go away, don't talk to me!

✳ Mama cries all the time.

✳ It's all Dad's fault. It's all Mom's fault. I want a normal family.

✳ I have a stomachache! My head hurts! Sometimes we might feel sick because we feel so sad.

✳ Money: Mom or Dad can't always buy everything you want like they used to do.

✳ Dad gets a new girlfriend. Mom gets a new boyfriend.

✳ Can I keep my pet? Can I get a pet? (A pet can be your best friend.)

✳ Now I have *two* rooms.

✳ Mom's mad at me all the time, or Dad's mad at me all the time. (He or she is *not* mad at you! They are hurting too. They are scared too. Everybody needs lots of hugs.)

✳ Divorce makes you grow up real fast. You have to learn things and get to know things children shouldn't have to know so fast.

✳ But *Dad* lets me do it . . . (Each house will probably have its own rules that you'll have to live with. Maybe Dad lets the kids stay up late and play video games all night; Mom makes them go to bed early. Dad lets them eat pizza all the time; Mom wants them to have a good meal.)

✳ New family for Dad or Mom. I don't want another Mother—I don't want another Dad! I hate that person they want to marry! Your mom will always be your mom, and your dad will always be your dad no matter what. So try not to worry if they marry someone else. Their love for you will not change.

✳ Maybe Mom and Dad will get back together again . . . ? (Don't allow yourself to get "false hopes." We live in the real world, and that probably will not happen.)

3.

Tammy Sue

Jim and I had been married for nine years when Tammy Sue Bakker came along. She weighed 6 pounds 5 ounces and had a full head of jet-black hair. She looked like a little Oriental doll baby with her beautiful slanted eyes. The doctor asked me who in our family was Asian. I never knew of an Asian relative, but that doesn't make it impossible that there was one. Family history can be so interesting and can come out in the most unexpected ways.

When Jim and I married, we immediately started to travel to different churches to minister. Jim preached and I sang. We also both worked with puppets. I was the voice of Susie Moppet and her best friend, Allie the Alligator. Jim swears to this day that I have a double or triple personality. Those two little puppets scared him to death. He talked to them in front of a little puppet house we had built, and he never knew what they were going to say or do. Those two puppets were as much a part of our ministry as we were. And not only the kids loved them, the adults did too.

We traveled on the road for five years when one night, in 1964, a man named Bill Garthwaite came to one of our services. He loved the puppets. He liked Jim and me, too, I guess, because he went back to his boss, who had a very small TV station, and told him about us. We never dreamed in a million years how that meeting would forever change our lives. We met with Pat Robertson, never intending to give up our by-now big ministry, reaching thousands. But Pat made Jim an offer he couldn't refuse. He said he wanted us to start a children's show with the puppets on his TV station, which at the time barely went around the block in Portsmouth, Virginia. But it was television, and that in itself was a big thing.

Jim told him yes, he and I would do a television show for children *if* Pat would allow him to also do another show he had dreamed about. Jim used to watch Johnny Carson, and he felt that Christians needed their own talk show. A place where Christian talent could perform and ministers could share their hearts with the people.

Pat agreed. A week or so later, we found ourselves building sets, cleaning out a room for an office, and putting together the first-ever Christian children's television show. It was called *Come On Over with Jim and Tammy*. A miracle began to happen before our very eyes. Kids were finding the show on the few TV sets that were around at that time. We began inviting them to come and be on the show with us. Well, of course someone had to bring them, and then the parents, too, began to get involved with Christian television. I will always think, be it right or wrong, that two little puppets had a lot to do with the success of Christian TV. Two little puppets and a lot of kids!

The Jim and Tammy Show, which it was later named, became the mother ship of the CBN television network. The show grew beyond our wildest imagination, and I think beyond what Pat ever thought could happen too. Telethons were born out of necessity. New stations were added, and a network was born. Then Jim reminded Pat of his promise. And Pat said, "Go for it!" He told Jim he could have as much airtime as he wanted for *The 700 Club,* which was the name of the first Christian talk show.

From the day it started I found myself more and more responsible for *The Jim and Tammy Show.* Jim was now immersed in his new show. Booking talent, acquiring guests who could talk on TV (some people can't, you know). The show started at 7 P.M. and sometimes—most of the time—went until two or three in the morning. The Rambos were among our first guests and sang for us up until we lost PTL TV—for about thirty years they were guests on Jim's shows. The Cameron family sang and preached for Jim as guests for about thirty years too. The Blackwood Brothers, and on and on and on.

I began to feel left out of Jim's life. His whole life became television. I saw him when we did the kid's show, then I went home and waited and waited and waited until he finally came in around three in the morning, dead tired. I had been begging him to let me have a baby for years, but he felt our life was too busy for children. I was becoming desperate to have a baby, someone I could love, someone to help take away the loneliness I faced day after day, night after night.

My persistence finally paid off. We could, finally, after eight years of marriage, start a family. I was so fortunate—I got pregnant almost immediately after we made the decision. I guess I was one of the happiest people alive. I went through my entire pregnancy on TV. The television audience was almost as excited as I was, I think. The crew teased me, calling our show *The Jim and Tammy Show*. At four feet eleven inches I was almost as wide as I was tall.

I did the show right up until the day I went into labor. It took me two days and nights of hard labor to finally bring Tammy Sue Bakker into the world, but it's the best work I've ever done. Nothing can compare with bringing a new life into the world. In those days you spent five days in the hospital. It was the longest five days of my life. All I wanted was to take my baby home, put her in the waiting bassinet by our bed, and start my life as a Mommy. That was all I ever wanted to be, and now at last the desire of my heart had come true.

She was born on March 2nd. I brought her home from the hospital on my birthday, March 7th. God has a wonderful sense of humor, doesn't He? He gave me the greatest birthday gift I have ever received! From the first day she was born, Tammy Sue slept through the night, which was a wonderful blessing from God. I would get scared in the middle of the night because she hardly ever cried. I would go and wake her up to make sure she was still alive. She was my heart. She became my life. I loved her as I have never loved another human being.

Television didn't matter anymore to me. But a week after I had Tammy Sue, I was back at work again. Grandma Fairchild had come to help me through the first few weeks. Grandma was my best friend in the whole world. She took care of Tammy Sue while I worked.

I will never forget one day, early in the morning, when Jim and I and Baby were still asleep. I felt a kiss on my cheek. It was

Grandma Fairchild. "Honey, it's time for Grandma to leave. The baby is starting to think I'm her mother." With that, Grandma was gone. I was alone again, but this time I really *wasn't* alone. It was me and a little tiny baby girl named Tammy Sue. She and I against the world.

I took her to work with me that day. I had to—we couldn't afford help, and I didn't want help anyway. We kept her on the set of the show in her bassinet for as long as she fit in it. Then we put a playpen on the set, and that's where she grew up. I was worried about her being with so many children all the time, worried that she would get sick. The doctor calmed my fears. He told me it would build up her immune system and she would be fine. He was right!

Tammy Sue learned to walk on television, she learned to talk on television. The crew became her extended family. Television cameras were just like the toys she pushed around. She would watch Jim and me duck under cameras, so when she toddled by a camera, she automatically ducked.

When the time came for us to leave Pat Robertson, we sold our house and bought a beautiful travel trailer. It was complete with a kitchen, living room, a full bedroom, and a full bath with tub. The tub is where we fixed a cozy bed for Susie, as we called her. She loved her bed in the tub. We traveled for a few months, a much-needed rest after nine years of hard work day and night. Jim and I got to know each other again, and we had the wonderful opportunity to spend all of our time with Susie. That was a happy few months for me. We were a family! A real family! Doing ordinary things.

But it was not to last for long. Jim drove toward our next destiny. We went from Portsmouth across the country to California. The promised land. It wasn't long before Jim met up with an old friend, his youth pastor from Muskegon, Michigan.

Paul Crouch and his wife, Jan, were a fun couple to be around, and we immediately bonded. Paul was working for another Christian TV station. In fact, it was a station that ran *The Jim and Tammy Show* and *The 700 Club*. Paul was tired of his job and suggested to Jim that they team up to do something together. Paul knew how to set up television and get Jim back on the air with his own show again. Jim was by now rested and restless to get back to work, and he had the knowledge of how to run everything once we were on the air. Jim would be the on-air person, and Paul would be the behind-the-scenes person and run the business end of things. Jim would be the president and Paul would be the vice president.

Jan and I really didn't care what they did. We were happy being together, learning to know each other as girlfriends. She had two boys and I had Susie, so we had something in common. Well, actually we had a lot in common. She loved to shop; I loved to shop. She loved flea markets; I loved flea markets. She loved makeup and wigs; I loved makeup and wigs. The Crouches suggested that we sell our mobile home and move into their garage, which was actually a beautiful extension of their home. We put the money we got from selling the trailer on a down payment for our own little house. I was so excited.

Once again Jim and I jumped in with both feet. We rented a building and began to renovate. The four of us, plus kids in tow. We worked day and night, along with volunteers Paul and Jan knew, to get that building ready to be a TV studio and offices. Paul and Jim worked well together. Jan and I had a ball together. It was a wonderful time.

We went on the air with great vigor. The show snowballed on us, and before we knew it we were a syndicated talk show all over the country again. We had a wonderful staff working with us. The money was scarce, but God always took care of us and somehow provided for our needs. We shared equally with our staff and workers whatever we could. And it worked.

But little did we know a storm was brewing. Brewing from within.

Paul and Jan saw the unprecedented success of the talk show and wanted to be more than just behind the scenes. One day Jan came up to Jim and said, "Jim, I think you should let Paul be president for a while now." You could have knocked Jim over with a feather. He could not believe what he was hearing. Paul had not given Jim any reason to suspect that all was not as it should be, or that he was unhappy in his position of business manager and vice president.

One day a few weeks later Paul came up to Jim. "Jim, we need to add to our board of directors." At that time it was just the four of us. He said, "I know some good pastors and business men that would love to be on our board."

Jim said, "Sure, Paul, whatever you think. You're the business manager and vice president, so do what you think needs to be done."

With that, Paul contacted the men he must have been talking to already, and new board members were added without Jim's thinking much of it. He was concentrating on the television show.

A few weeks later Paul came to Jim's office. "I need to talk to you, Jim. The board of directors have voted you out. You are no longer working here."

It was as if a bolt of lightning hit Jim and me and our staff of faithful workers. We began to pack our office in a fog. We could not believe what Paul had done. We were best friends! We trusted Paul and Jan. We loved Paul and Jan. *Why?* What would we tell the people? Who would take over the TV show? What would happen to our staff?

Well, it wasn't long before those questions were answered. We left, and the entire staff walked out with us unbidden. Paul and Jan took over our TV show. We stayed in California for a few weeks, as we had no idea what to do next. The staff met at our house every day as if we were all still working. But instead of working, we prayed and prayed and prayed. God, what are we going to do? Any money or food we had was again divided equally among all of us, and somehow we lived.

One of our partners in the TV show owned a restaurant. A fantastic restaurant that served buffet-style. She let all of us, about twenty as I remember, eat there every day for free. Her name was Herta Backland, and she has since gone to be with the Lord. What a crown she must have received!

People came from everywhere, writing us checks that were not asked for, to help our families until we could relocate. In spite of broken promises, broken hearts, and losing our ministry, it was not as awful as you would think. We all had to sell our homes, figure out what to do with furniture, etc. As one house would sell, that family would move in with us or with another staff person whose home had not yet sold.

We never heard a word from Paul and Jan Crouch.

One day Jim got a call from Charlotte, North Carolina. Our shows had run there, and they had heard what happened to us. They said that a huge group of people had been praying for weeks that we would start something in Charlotte. They invited Jim to come and speak at a huge rally.

He did—and once again, it was destiny. Our lives were to change forever.

Jim left to start Christian TV in Charlotte. The staff and I stayed behind, hired trucks to move our personal possessions across the country, and got the houses sold. The relief was overwhelming!

We had wonderful people working with us in Charlotte. Jim and all of us working together took a small building that formerly sold easy chairs and transformed it into a TV studio and offices. Volunteers came to help us daily, as Jim Bakker once again hosted a Christian talk show. He was the best there has ever been—he was anointed to do that job. It was his calling. His vision. He loved the people and carried a genuine burden for them. And those people watching the TV show became a part of our family. A family of thousands and thousands.

Once again the show began to snowball. We quickly outgrew the facilities, and were forced to take a huge leap of faith to acquire land and, for the first time, build. But Jim had enough faith for all of us. God led Jim and we followed. Followed him into a whirlwind of unmitigated success.

We built an unbelievable new television facility. Jim fashioned it after Colonial Williamsburg. People came from all around the world to be a part of the ministry.

And once again I was not a part of Jim Bakker's life. Or I should say I *felt* that I was not a part of Jim's life. I wanted another baby desperately. Tammy Sue was now five years old, and I didn't want her to be an only child. So I was elated when Jamie Charles Bakker was born. He was such a beautiful baby, his little head perfectly formed (I had to have a cesarean section). Now we had our girl and our boy.

The night my water broke, I could not get ahold of Jim. We

did not have cell phones in those days. It was about 2 A.M., and he was still at the TV studio, working. I was frantic. I pictured him in a ditch, dead beside the road. We lived way out in the country. I did not have a car and felt very isolated. Why didn't he call? He could at least call. Please God!

At 2:30, Jim walked into the house. I was relieved—and angry. Anger won out, and for the first time in our marriage I locked myself in the guest room and slept alone. Slept alone for about three or four hours, until I told him we needed to go to the hospital. Jim took me in and stayed until he had to go do the TV show. I told him I would be fine.

Jamie was born just before the show was over. Jim had left the show a few minutes early, leaving Jim Moss and Uncle Henry Harrison to host. The doctor called the TV studio about a minute before they went off the air, and they were able to announce to an excited TV audience that we had just had a baby boy. A TV studio full of people were screaming and clapping while Jim was in his car on the way to the hospital, unaware of what had just happened. What a surprise when he got there and found out we had a wonderful, darling baby boy.

The happiest time of my life was when I was able to be with Tammy Sue and Jamie and be a Mom. I loved taking care of them. But I, like Jim, had a calling in life, and that calling followed me around like a little puppy barking at my heels, begging to be picked up.

After Jamie was born, we realized we had to have some help. Jim knew I was feeling left out of his television life, and he made me co-host of the TV show for the first time. It was bittersweet. I was happy to be back at Jim's side doing television again, but I hated not being able to be with my children. We had wonderful, competent people who worked for us. The lady who helped me with the kids was the best. She loved them as if they were her own. And she loved us. I can still see her so clearly. Her name was Johnnie Mae. When I came home so tired I could hardly walk after a long day's work, she would say, "Sit down, Mrs. Bakker, let me fix you something to eat." She would soothe my frayed nerves with her gentle spirit and kind hands of service. She heard everything that ever happened in our home. She knew we were a normal family with normal problems. She heard the raised voices of frustration. She was used to hearing the phone ring and us saying, "Johnnie Mae, we won't be home till late tonight. Can you stay?" Never once did she say no. She saw the tears, she knew the struggles of our marriage, yet never once did she betray us. We trusted Johnnie Mae with our very lives, and she never once disappointed us. Tammy Sue and Jamie loved Johnnie Mae.

> Fear thou not; for I am with thee: be not dismayed: for I am thy God; I will strengthen thee; yea, I will help thee; yea, I will uphold thee with the right hand of my righteousness.
>
> ISAIAH 41:10

Tammy Sue was growing up before our very eyes. I think she was born grown up. She always had unbelievably good sense, even as a tiny child. She attended the school at Heritage USA where the PTL television studio was located. (We created Heritage USA after we outgrew the Williamsburg village facilities.) She was a happy child, totally occupied with her school and her friends and all the social events that took place at Heritage USA. She learned from the very best how to be a lady, how to dress, how to act. She never knew anything but TV and lots and lots of people. Six million people visited Heritage USA the last year we were there, so she was used to having aunts and uncles and Moms and Dads everywhere. They all took care of Tammy Sue. She was always everyone's little girl.

In spite of all the pomp and ceremony and grandeur, she was never affected. She was good and kind and sweet to everyone she came in contact with, even when they insisted on hugging and taking pictures and intruding on whatever she was doing at the time. Still, one thing I heard her say many times was, "I wish our family was just normal." I think she longed for a Dad who worked nine to five and a Mom who was home when she got home from school. She longed for a vacation that didn't include TV crews and staff. I think she wished that we weren't so well known and could go places without being recognized.

I don't really know what Tammy Sue based her idea of a normal family on, because she had never known life any other way. I suppose she based it on the way her friends lived, which was not that normal, either, as they all worked for us, traveled with us, and did so many of the same things we did. How she stayed so grounded and down to earth I don't know. But she has. And I don't know why she never got bitter and hard when she saw people she loved all her life betray our family. I think it is her love for God and the teaching that she has soaked up. She is grounded in the Lord.

Of all the suffering our family has been through, I would say Tammy Sue has suffered the most. She ran away from all the terrible hurt only to realize that she carried the hurt with her. After we had lost PTL and Heritage USA, we were staying in California. We had a small home, a place where we could get away to once in a while. The news media had plagued us for days. Their satellite relays and trucks lined the entire block in front of our house. There was no way to leave our home without running into fifty news people. It was so awful, especially for the kids. The media followed us everywhere we went, even if it was to the grocery store. We could not set foot outside our gated entrance.

One particular day, I couldn't find Tammy Sue. We looked everywhere for her. Her little car was sitting in the driveway, so we went to look in her car. On the car we found a note. It read: *Mom and Dad, I'm on an airplane going back to Charlotte.* One of the staff members whom we had trusted had paid for a ticket so Tammy Sue could run away. (This was the same staff member who went to jail for not paying taxes on a large sum of money. Coincidentally, a large amount of PTL money was unaccounted for. The man never was charged with embezzlement, but there were suspicions.)

We were devastated! She had a boyfriend in Charlotte, who was a busboy in a hotel. They had been talking on the phone, and he told her she could live with his mother. Tammy Sue liked his mom, so she decided to go.

Her life from that point on became a living nightmare. My heart aches unbearably when I think of how she suffered. She wound up living in a small trailer house Jim bought her. It was out in the middle of a field, out in the country. She didn't have a car, and two babies later she suffered a nervous breakdown. (I am compacting this because I know that someday she will write her own book.)

I thought she would never come out of that breakdown. It was the worst thing I have ever been through. Here I was living in California while she was in Charlotte, and I had no money to go to her. I stayed on the phone with her night and day. I have never prayed so much and so hard in my entire life. I made up my mind that the devil was *not* going to take my beautiful daughter, and I came against his power over her body in Jesus' name. Kelly Lein, a friend Tammy Sue had grown up with, was with her. Kelly's mom, Joyce, had worked for us for years and was one of my best friends. They were praying women, and they, too, came against the power of Satan, who was trying to destroy Tammy Sue. Her two little boys were with their dad and were not allowed to see their own mother as she struggled through the worst point in her life.

Thank God that Jim was there for her. We were divorced by this time, and he had just gotten out of prison. He went to where she was staying and slept on the floor by her bed for nights, not daring to leave her alone. Everyone thought that she was going to commit suicide. The doctors put her on medication, but it didn't seem to help. She cried and cried for days, as if her heart was going to break. She cut herself with any sharp object she could get her hands on. Some people wanted to put her in an institution, but I screamed over the phone to Jim: *Don't you dare let them do that to Tammy Sue. You take care of her.* And God bless his heart, he did! Jim and I were on the phone to each other every day.

After much prayer and much love from her loyal girlfriends, her dad, and me, Tammy Sue began to get better. God spoke to me that I needed to move back to Charlotte to be with my daughter. Roe, my new husband, had just gotten out of prison himself, and he flew back to Charlotte to find a house for us. He found one, and within a couple of months I was back home again, with my daughter and her two precious boys, James and Jonathan. I went with her to a lawyer and she got a divorce.

Since then we have been on quite a journey, she and I. But we have become best friends. There is nothing more wonderful in the world than having your best friend as your daughter. I thank God every day for my beautiful, giving, talented daughter. She is one of the greatest singers I have ever heard, and she is anointed to preach the Gospel of Jesus Christ. She is ministering in churches all over this country and has just signed a record contract. Her two boys are happy, well-adjusted kids. They love their dad and they love their mom, who have shared custody. And then there's always Grandma's house, where they have their own room they decorated themselves. They have great taste! They call Grandma and Grandpa Roe's house "the neutral place, like Switzerland." And when they're with me I can't get the smile off my face.

I don't know what would have happened to Tammy Sue had I not moved back to Charlotte. I refuse to let my mind go there. All I know is that I've never been so happy in my life, to be here with my daughter and my two grandchildren. Jamie Charles and his wife, Amanda, are not too far away—just a day's drive, in Atlanta, where he is a minister. For the first time in nearly forty years I am peaceful, my mind is at rest, and I can look back and thank God for bringing us all through. My song I sang for so many years on television, "You Can Make It!" has special meaning these days. Because with the help of God and faith that would not allow us to give up, we did! We made it!

4.

Marriage and Divorce

It was a beautiful day in Atlanta, Georgia. A large group of family and friends were gathering in front of the historic old church where my son, Jamie Charles Bakker, was about to marry the girl of his dreams. He and I and Roe Messner stood there quietly talking, watching what was going on around us. Jamie looked so handsome in his tuxedo, towering above his mom. My heart was singing for my son. His father, Jim Bakker, was already in the church preparing the wedding ceremony. We were waiting for Tammy Sue to arrive. When she got there our family, as Jamie knew it, would be complete: Dad, Mom, Jamie Charles, and Tammy Sue.

I don't know why, but I felt strangely alone standing there that day. I was deep in thought when Jamie touched my arm.

"Mom, it's time to go in."

I took my husband's arm and we followed Jamie and his groomsmen into the foyer of the church. People were being seated inside. I could hear laughter in a room not far away, where the bride and her bridesmaids were. I peeked in, and there stood the most beautiful bride I had ever seen. It took my breath away. The excitement was palpable. There she stood, waiting for the sounds of the church organ, a sign for the bridal procession to begin.

Amanda and Jamie had been dating for nearly two years. They had chosen to remain virgins until their wedding night. They did not keep that fact a secret.

I felt a tug on my arm. It was the usher.

"Time to go sit down," he said, smiling.

He ushered Roe and me to the front of the church. I felt as if I were watching a movie as the bridal party filed in and took their proper places in the front of the church, my handsome son, my baby, among them.

Then my ex-husband, Jim Bakker, took his place. Everyone stood to the opening strains of "Here Comes the Bride." My eyes filled with tears of joy as Amanda, in white, walked down the aisle to her Jamie. A beautiful voice filled the church. It was Tammy Sue singing "Amazing Grace."

So everyone else in our family had a part in the wedding, while I sat there in the front row. I felt so left out, as if I didn't belong. Yet I was so grateful that Jim was performing the ceremony. I would not have had it any other way. It was the right thing for Jim to do. And I was so proud of my two children, there for each other at such an important time of their lives.

Then why did I feel so alone? As if I had been abandoned? Why did I long so to be a part of my son's wedding, as his dad was? I had teased Jamie that I, too, was an ordained minister. Now I felt as though I had died and was watching the ceremony from Heaven.

And then the ceremony was over, the vows said, and they all

started down the aisle. That was when Jamie announced, "I would like for my mom to stand up."

Roe pushed me to my feet. My precious son stopped everything, put his arm around me, kissed me, and said, "I love you, Mom."

I will forever hold that moment in my heart. They didn't forget me, after all. I wasn't left out in Jamie's heart. I felt so guilty for thinking or feeling that I was.

I never told anyone about that feeling. No one would ever have known. I only tell it now because perhaps it will help you to hear it. Maybe you've been in that place, too, with those feelings.

> You can't stop a bird from flying over your head, but you don't need to let it build a nest in your hair!

Divorce jumps up and bites you in the butt when you least expect it. I know that is the very reason God says He hates divorce. His perfect will for us is to stay married. God created the family unit, and divorce breaks that unit and forever changes it. In most cases, one member of the family will always be missing for the important occasions. Everyone has to plan two Christmases, two of everything—one at Dad's house, one at Mom's.

I do not regret my divorce. My husband, Roe, and I are unbelievably happy. Still, we have both paid a price for our happiness, even if we do it willingly. We have two happy families instead of one.

Thirteen Things to Remember About Divorce

1. Make sure it's not a spur-of-the-moment decision—that it is well thought out. Be absolutely sure the marriage can no longer survive. It took me three years to finally make the decision to divorce Jim. Three years of praying, talking to Christian psychologists, talking to my friends who knew both Jim and me, and looking within myself, deciding what I could live with for the rest of my life and what I could not. I did not take divorce lightly. I had not taken my marriage vows lightly. I considered *everything*.

2. What about your children? Are you prepared for how your decision will affect them? Jamie was sixteen and Tammy Sue was already married with children when Jim and I were divorced. Jamie called me the night before I was to marry Roe and told me I was going straight to Hell. I knew what his reaction was going to be and expected it, but it still cut my heart to pieces. It took time, but he now loves Roe and we are very close.

3. Are you prepared to hear the opinions of other people? People can be very cruel. My dearest friends tried to talk me out of getting a divorce. Some of them turned their backs on

me and did not speak to me for years. But the old adage "Time heals all wounds" proved true for me.

4. Are you prepared for the financial upheaval divorce can cause? What belongs to whom? Alimony? Child support? Who gets custody of the children?

5. Are you prepared, if you remarry, for a second family? Are you prepared to face an ex-wife or ex-husband? If there are children, especially young children, are you prepared to share your new spouse with his or her family obligations?

6. Are you prepared for memories shared that *you* don't share? I was married for over thirty years to Jim. Roe was married for over thirty years to his ex-wife. We have two separate sets of memories that we did not experience together. When my kids and I get together, we share our family memories. When Roe and his kids get together, they share theirs. Stories of days gone by that will live forever.

7. Are you prepared for an entirely new life?

8. Are you prepared to keep your mouth shut? And not to compare your new spouse to the way your ex-spouse did things?

9. Are you prepared to be alone if you do not remarry?

10. Be prepared for your and your ex-spouse's mutual friends to choose sides. Now that you're single, *(continued)*

Thirteen Things to Remember About Divorce *(cont'd)*

you will feel left out of couples' events. And be prepared for women to be jealous of you and men to flirt with you—even old friends. Things totally change!

11. Be prepared to feel guilty for a long, long time. Guilt is a part of divorce. Guilt over the way your kids feel, guilt over anything that goes wrong. You will constantly be asking yourself, "What if . . . ?" I had to refuse to let my mind dwell on what ifs. There's an old saying: "You can't stop a bird from flying over your head, but you don't need to let it build a nest in your hair!" The same goes for thoughts. Chase them away and get on with your new life! You must get the what ifs and if onlys out of your vocabulary! They will ruin your life if you let them. And only *you* can control what you're thinking. Be stronger than the bad thoughts. You can! Choose to be a conqueror! Ask God to help you. The Bible says to think on things that are pure and good.

12. Do *not* fight in front of your children. It's not their problem. It's your problem. Don't burden them with your pain; they'll have enough of their own to deal with.

13. Be honest with your children about the divorce if they're old enough to understand—but stick to the bare facts, don't embellish. And once you have explained, leave it there. Don't badmouth your ex. Don't forget: In most cases the children love you both, so don't force them to take sides. Don't be guilty of poisoning your child's mind against your ex.

5.

Christmas

It's Christmas time, my favorite time of the year. My house is so beautifully decorated from stem to stern. Beautiful greenery and lights around the doors and windows, two Christmas trees, candles in all the windows of my typical Carolina house. Deer stand in our front yard, their mechanical heads going back and forth, their bodies covered in white lights. The bushes that surround the house are also covered in white lights; lighted, bigger-than-life candy canes line the walk to the front door. Everything looks like Christmas!

I've been shopping and wrapping gifts for weeks, for friends and people I know who would not have a Christmas gift if it were not for us. I've even hosted the neighborhood Christmas party where all us ladies got together, exchanged ornaments, ate, talked and laughed. And then we ate some more. I've made my Christmas fudge twice now. I've had the Bose blasting Christmas carols. We've even been to the church Christmas program with good friends. I've written and sent out dozens of Christmas cards and received dozens back. Gifts fill the once-empty space under our tree in the den. It's Christmas!

But as hard as I try, I can't seem to get my mind to accept the fact that this year it's as though I'm playing some kind of game, going through motions I don't feel. I think I'm sad.

I talked with my husband about it. We came to the conclusion that age might have something to do with my feelings, or lack of, this year. He says the older you get, the harder it is to truly enjoy the season that was once so special to us. But if that's the case, that in itself is very sad. I never want to be one of those older people who have seen it all, heard it all, and had it all, who no longer have the ability to get excited over things, and no longer want to make things special. I want the child in me to endure, to stay alive! I want to be excited about things. And in some way, I believe that is a choice, as are most things in life.

My mind keeps wanting to think about Christmases past. When the whole family was together. When Mom and Dad and Grandma and Grandpa Fairchild and Aunt Gin and Donny and Judy were still alive. Donny, my brother, and Aunt Gin, my mentor, both died this last year. My sister Judy and my dad died the year before. My mom died a couple of years before them, and Grandma and Grandpa Fairchild have been gone now many Christmases. I miss them!

We were a poor family, but we never knew it. At least us kids didn't. I never once heard Mom complain about the things she didn't have. She just acted like she had them.

I miss the way Mom decorated our old house. Everything that could be decorated was decorated! I think I'm like my mom in that respect. She didn't go to the party, she *was* the party. She made everything so much fun. Our house didn't have a fireplace, but that didn't stop Mom. She went out and bought a life-sized fireplace made from heavy cardboard. Then she bought a flickering cardboard fire to go in it. She hung our stockings from it and decorated the mantel, just the way you would the real thing. We kids, the eight of us, would turn out all the lights and sit in front of that fireplace by the hour. It was so cozy!

I miss Daddy and the boys dragging the Christmas tree into the house. It would be covered with snow and fill the entire house with the wonderful aroma of pine. Mom would let us all help decorate the tree. She filled it with lots and lots of lights, those big old-fashioned red, green, blue, and gold ones. Then she would add those wonderful bubbling lights, and cover the tree in sparkling tinsel.

She made a Christmas wonderland out of our plain old dining room table. It was complete with miniature houses, trees, cars, people, skating rinks—everything lighted, of course. And all placed on a huge blanket of artificial snow, another part of Christmas that delighted us kids.

My favorite gift I ever received was a little kitchen set that really worked. The sink dripped water out of the faucet, the fridge door had a light when it opened, and the little stove glowed. I was in Heaven! And, of course, I always got a baby doll to love all year long. I have often thought that if I could somehow live over one day of my life it would be one of those Christmases together.

Then, too, I miss all the Christmases I had when my own children were small, and I was doing for them what Mom did for us kids. I miss having small children around; I miss seeing that special wonderment that they have, the light in their eyes, the laughter, the sound of little feet running excitedly through the house asking, "When can we open our presents?" I miss my two kids!

This year, Jamie Charles has his own wife, Amanda. They're having their own Christmas, which I know is so exciting for them. Tammy Sue will be home, for which I am so thankful. She will be bringing James and Jonathan to our house Christmas Eve. She can't pick them up until 8 P.M. from her ex-husband. His family also opens gifts on Christmas Eve. Then they'll go home with Tammy Sue and celebrate Christmas Eve again, with just Mom. They'll have a wonderful time together, in their own way. One generation following another.

So why am I sad? Some grandparents never get to be with their grandchildren and children on holidays. I am so blessed! Maybe it's because of the emptiness I'll feel when I wave goodbye to them as they walk down the lighted candy-cane path. I'm a part of their lives, yet I'm not. I have to let them go, have to allow them to decide when they come and see me and when they have other things that are more important to do. My heart knows I may not see them for weeks, even though we live in the same town. I miss being with my children, I think I miss being in control—a selfish feeling, I know. But I think it's a feeling that's normal for parents who were close to their children.

I think I miss my youth. I don't think I've ever accepted the fact that I'm not young anymore. I feel so young inside! My grandma once said, "I'm a young person in an old body, honey." And she was always young at heart, as were Mom and Aunt Gin.

I will get through Christmas, and I will get through it with joy. I have determined in my heart to do that. I must focus on what Christmas is really about. It's not about the family being together, it's not about gifts or big meals: It's about the birth of Jesus. It's His birthday we're celebrating.

So, sadness, fly away! Joy to the world, the Lord has come, let earth receive its King. Happy birthday, Jesus! Happy birthday!

6.

Just One
More Time

August 11, 1992. I was watching a rerun of *The Waltons* on TV. They had just had a fire in their home and lost everything. Mr. Walton was working, trying to rebuild the house. John Boy walked up to his discouraged dad, who said, "John Boy, this isn't working, there's something wrong. I can't get this done. I'm trying to build it exactly as it was before."

John Boy looked at his frustrated dad and said, "Dad, you can't have everything exactly as it was before. You must move on, go forward. This house is this house, that house was that house."

Sometimes I feel sad for what was. I find myself wanting to go back to the safety of that time. The house in Tega Cay, the TV program, the set that was always there, the band, the singers, the TV crew. Phoebe Conway in the Green Room, my office with its beautiful cream-and-pink-flowered couch and my white desk.

Sometimes I want to go home to Johnnie Mae, our housekeeper, working in the kitchen. Just one more time I'd like to look across the table at the kids, Tammy Sue and Jamie Charles, as children. Just one more time I'd like to go outside and sit on the dock next to the big old houseboat our family so enjoyed. I'd like to call the kids one more time and tell them to get on the boat, we're going for a ride.

Just one more time I'd like to grill hamburgers around our pool with our neighbors Judy and Blair Bycura. I'd like to see all our kids together again, splashing us as they dive off the diving board, asking, "When will the food be ready, Mom?" I'd like to go sit at Judy's table and eat her homemade beans and cornbread, just one more time.

> Life is what's coming, not what was.

Just one more time I'd like to put my arms around Max and Mindy, Blair and Judy's big St. Bernard dogs. We felt so safe with them there, protecting us. Just once more I'd like to walk back through all the rooms of our big old house. The media called it a mansion. I laugh when I think about that! It was just an old house we worked on and added to until it fit the needs of our family.

I'd like to put Jamie Charles to bed in his cute little room one more time, and put the toy he was afraid of outside the door of his room. I wish I could spend one more day in my bedroom. Could walk into my dressing room one more time. I'd like to sit one more time on Susie's bed and watch her get ready to go somewhere, to talk to her about a bigger closet, to see her little playhouse and play with the rabbit she kept on her porch.

One more time I'd like to wrap presents in the den downstairs at the big table. Would like to remind the kids not to look as they walk through the room, so excited about Christmas coming. I'd like to lie in my tanning bed in the exercise room one more time. Just once more I'd like to sit at the baby grand piano in our pretty living room, listening to Mike Murdock sing me new songs he's written for my next album. I'd like to taste one of the brownies that Johnnie Mae would bring to the piano as we were working there.

I'd like, just one more time, to go out into the atrium and see my birds again. I miss them so much. I'd like to feel Fancy, the dove, land on my head, and hear her laugh. I'd like to hear Polly Parrot squawk a hello, begging me to come over to her cage. I'd like to hear the parakeets singing as they fly around free through the trees in the atrium.

One more time I'd like to see Tinkerbell, our big white cat, walk by, feel the softness of her body as she lies on the bed next to me. The weight of her as she lies on my feet when I am in bed not feeling well. She seemed to know when I wasn't feeling well.

Just once more I'd like to walk through my big closet and wonder what in the world was I going to do with all these clothes! Or look in my shoe closet, created for my size fives.

One more time I'd like to walk on that deep, soft, dark green carpet I thought was so pretty. I'd like to sit in the deep mauve chair by the fireplace in my bedroom one more time. Just one more time, I'd like to drive out of the driveway of the Tega Cay house and hear the guards say, "Goodbye, Tammy, have a good day," on my way to do our TV show.

But, as John Boy said, you can't go back. Things can never again be exactly as they were. Nothing ever stays the same. Life goes on and we must go on with life. There is such safety in things that are familiar. But growth only comes through change—and that's a good thing! Albeit a bit sad.

7.

Aunt Gin

She was a tiny little lady, weighing in at about one hundred pounds. She was so cute and so full of energy. She was sharp-witted and at times a bit on the salty side. She could shut you up quickly with just a look. She had beautiful hair, long and fluffy, that she rinsed in vinegar after every washing. She had the shiniest hair I've ever seen. She had a very womanly shape, an old-fashioned hourglass figure with a tiny waist. She loved clothes, which she designed and made herself. She loved fur coats; living in Minnesota, they kept her little frame warm. She loved rings. She wore them on almost every finger. And she loved me.

She was my mother's sister, my aunt Virginia Fairchild. I called her Aunt Gin.

I think since the day I was born I belonged more to her than I did to Mom. She never married. She worked at F. W. Woolworth's, where she handled all the money for fifty years. She had a darling apartment she lived in for fifty years, and for fifty years I was "her kid."

She made life very special for me. I was the oldest of eight kids, and that's all my life would have consisted of had it not been for her. She knew I worked hard at home helping Mom, so she made me a priority in her life. I took my first tub bath at her house; she gave me my first permanent. As I wiggled and complained that she was pulling my hair, she said that it takes pains to be beautiful, and if I was not willing to pay the price she'd stop right there. So I shut up. Aunt Gin's bark was worse than her bite. The minute we were finished, she and I would get our coats on and walk to the nearest bakery, where we would stuff ourselves with fresh jelly-filled doughnuts.

She took me to church with her every Sunday. We went to the Mission Covenant Church in South International Falls, Minnesota, about three blocks from my house. I loved church, especially the singing. Aunt Gin had a beautiful, clear voice. When the whole church sang, you could hear one voice over all the rest, ringing clear and true. My aunt Gin. She encouraged my natural love of singing and soon had me singing solos in church. She would play the piano for me. She taught me how to enunciate and to project my voice. None of this sweet, soft singing for her. Belt it out, kid! If you're going to sing, *sing*. And I did. And I still am.

Every Thanksgiving, without fail, Aunt Gin and I would walk across the border to Canada to shop. And we always bought my mom a set of salt and pepper shakers, which she collected. We'd walk home, after hours of shopping, into our warm, snugly house filled with the aroma of turkey and pumpkin pie, and with my seven siblings, and Grandma and Grandpa Fairchild. We'd all gather around the tables (plural), thirteen of us, and eat until we could eat no more. Mom left the food out and we snacked all afternoon on leftovers. And no, we never got food poisoning.

Aunt Gin taught me all the "girl stuff." Manners, how to shave under my arms without bleeding to death, how to shave my legs, the importance of being well groomed and polite at all times. She taught me *never, ever* to tell a lie, to sit with my legs in a ladylike position, and to stand up and sit straight.

She gave me my first job when I was barely fifteen, at Woolworth's, of course. She taught me to be punctual. In her book there was *never* any excuse for being late. After all, I was her niece, and it would reflect on her if I were to be late. So I'd ride my bike to work, it would be zero degrees outside, my legs purple with the cold, pedaling as if my very life depended on it, to get to Woolworth's on time. I never wanted to incur Aunt Gin's wrath, that *look*.

She also taught me about money, not that I ever had any. You see, almost every dime I made at Woolworth's went for purses or rings. I wonder who I took after? One day, I'll never forget it, she called me into her office. I walked up to the locked door, she rang the buzzer, I turned the knob and pushed and was in. She had that look on her face, tinged by a bit of a smile. She said, "Now, Tammy Faye, you must stop spending all your money on purses, or you won't have any money to put in them." Then she proceeded to tell me that she was going to start a savings account for me. Every week from that day she took money out of my paycheck and put it away for me.

Five years later I wanted to go to Bible college, but I was sure my parents couldn't afford to send me. Once again, Aunt Gin called me into her office.

"Honey, you have enough money saved to pay your tuition.

You get a job, and that will give you spending money. If after that you still need extra, don't worry, I'll help you."

And I did just as she said. I enrolled in North Central Bible College and got me a job at the Three Sisters clothing store. Aunt Gin never wrote me without including "that little extra." She taught me good work ethics—I was number-one salesgirl at the Three Sisters. And I was *never* late.

This morning Roe walked into our bedroom and said, "Honey, Aunt Gin died last night."

What do you do when you hear those words? How do you keep your heart from jumping out of your chest? How am I going to live without my aunt Gin? Who am I going to call when I need her advice? I cannot even imagine living the rest of my life without hearing her clear voice saying my name. The Minnesota part of her enunciating each word she spoke. She never dropped a "g." How can I live without hearing her say, "I love you, honey," as we hung up the phone? She knew me since I was born. She loved me unconditionally. She never once seemed to notice my makeup or my eyelashes. She just noticed *me*.

I love you, Aunt Gin. How I will miss you. But I know where you are, and I'll be along one of these days. The angels in Heaven's choir will welcome your beautiful clear voice, and when they sing next time one voice will be heard above all the others. Hey, I recognize that voice—it's my aunt Gin!

With love,
Your Kid

P.S. You won't have to shovel snow this winter, Aunt Gin!

8.

February 19, 2002

It was a day like any other day. I jumped out of bed and made it up quickly, putting all my dolls and pillows in their places. I got dressed and ran downstairs to drink my Slim-Fast breakfast. The sun was shining, so I decided to go shopping. I parked my car a long distance from the shopping center so I could get my ten thousand steps in. They say that's how many steps you need to walk a day to maintain a good weight and stay healthy. I remember talking to a stranger and saying how wonderful it was to see the sunshine again and what a happy day it was. Funny that I should remember it being such a happy day. I arrived home about the middle of the afternoon, and Roe asked me if I would like to go out to dinner and a movie. That sounded like fun, as we had been busy traveling and working and had not had much time for relaxation.

The phone rang like it does many times a day, and Roe called me in the bedroom. It was Ruthie, my youngest sister. We had been writing back and forth from Minnesota, and I had sent her a gift, so her call seemed normal.

I could immediately tell she'd been crying. Her next words changed my life forever.

"Tam, something awful has happened to Donny."

My heart nearly stopped! I had just talked to my brother a few days ago. We had not seen each other in such a long time, and one day I sat down and wrote him, telling him how much I missed him and how we needed to plan a time to get together again. He called me a few days later, and we laughed and talked as if we saw each other every day. Donny and I were the only children of my mom and dad, Rachel and Carl LaValley. They got a divorce and both remarried. My mom had six more children and my dad had eight more. But Don and I were especially close. Now Ruthie was telling me that something terrible had happened to him.

I held my breath, afraid to say anything. She continued, "Tam, Don is dead. He died today. He and his wife were taking their usual walk with their dog, laughing and talking, and Don fell to the ground. He was dead when he hit the ground."

Dead at fifty-seven. A massive heart attack.

Roe could hear me crying from his office. He came running to find out what was wrong. In my life I thought the worst things that could possibly happen had already happened to me. I was wrong! When I heard the words "Don is dead," I felt as if someone had shot a twelve-inch hole in my chest. A hole that may get smaller with time but will never be completely healed.

How do you prepare yourself for the funeral of someone you love so much? This was different from Mom's funeral. Different from my two dads' funerals. I knew they could not live as long as me. But Don was *younger* than me. My little brother!

I got on the airplane, for the first time in my life not afraid to fly. I didn't care. I was on my way to see my brother again, for the last time. I would have run all the way to Minnesota if that were the only way to get there. I was numb, my heart panic-stricken. Could my heart stand seeing my brother in a casket? My good-looking, funny, fun, talented brother? I would only know the answer to that question when I got there and had to face it.

After landing in Minneapolis, we drove three hundred miles to International Falls. I wore my red pantsuit to the funeral. Red for courage. Donny would have liked that I didn't wear black. I wish I could have filled the church with balloons. Flowers just didn't seem appropriate for such a fun-loving man, who loved life and lived it to the fullest. Flowers die, and I didn't want to be around anything else that I knew was going to die. All of us relatives were standing there, each lost in our own thoughts.

Then they brought in the casket. I guess that is the saddest sight I have ever seen. It was a long, kind of gray casket, the kind they use when a person is going to be cremated following the funeral. I wished it could have been grand-looking. Beautiful, shiny, masculine-looking wood, the kind that rich men are buried in. It looked so desolate and lonely to me.

Two men wheeled it down the aisle of the little church we'd all grown up in and placed it in front of the altar. Then the moment I had been dreading became a reality. They opened the casket lid and there was my Donny. I literally ran to him! "I'm here, Don, I'm here. I love you, Donny," I whispered. I couldn't take my eyes off him. In desperation, I tried to put in my memory everything about him. His beautiful skin, his handsome, young-looking face, his rugged, manly hands, his well-trimmed beard, graying a bit I noticed, his hair cut short. We looked a lot alike, Don and me. They had dressed him in a dark blue shirt and jeans. Beside him was his favorite hat, a cowboy hat. Leaning up against the communion table was his guitar and a picture of him next to his pickup truck with a cigarette in his hand. He would have loved it! And in an Assembly of God church, no less! A smile crossed my grieving face.

> The tragedy of life is not that it ends so soon, but that we wait so long to begin it.

I don't know what Emily Post would say about taking pictures at a funeral, but I did. I *had* to. I put my brother's hat on and cocked it to the side. His wife said, "Tammy, that's exactly the way he wore it!" I know it really didn't happen, but I swear I saw him grin that crooked grin of his when I did that. I kept holding onto his hands, wishing I could impart some of my warmth into them. I picked up his guitar and placed it next to the casket. Why didn't I know that my brother was a wonderful, talented guitar player, and that his dream was one day to start a country band of his own? Why didn't I know that he loved music as much as I did?

At every funeral we all make a pact to write, call, get together more often. When we say it, we really mean it. But we never do. Our lives keep spinning in different directions. And somehow we know the next time we meet again will be in that little church at another funeral.

I know that my brother went to his real home, Heaven. And I know that he is up there talking and laughing with those loved ones who have gone on before. That knowledge helps me to live in peace, but it doesn't dull the terrible aching in my heart.

It doesn't heal the hole that will be there forever. And it doesn't stop me from looking up toward Heaven and saying, with tears streaming down my face, "God, *I want my brother back.*"

I love you, Donald Charles LaValley! Rest in peace. I don't know when, but I'll be along one of these days. See you then, Don.

Love,

Sis

P.S. Donny was cremated following the funeral. It was his wish. The pictures I took I will always treasure.

9.

Patty Goes Home

My girlfriend died today. My beautiful, vibrant, redheaded, funny girlfriend. She was just fifty-six years old, way too young to say goodbye to.

I talked on the phone to her just last week. She was in the hospital. It was her first day out of intensive care. She had suffered a light stroke after having not felt well for about a week. I was relieved to hear her talking and laughing and asking me for the thousandth time in a year, "When are you going to come and see me?" I never dreamed when I told her I loved her, and she told me that she loved me more, that it would be the last time. Patty couldn't die! She was just too full of life. She just loved life too much. She was a survivor.

You see, about five years ago Patty discovered a lump in her breast. She was told by her doctor that she had breast cancer. Because of extensive chemotherapy she nearly died twice after her surgery. I'll never forget going to Tulsa, Oklahoma, to visit her. Her hair was all gone. She was so thin you could almost see through her, but as sick as she was, there she was in that hospital bed, all her makeup perfect and a leopard turban on her head. Even in her severely weakened condition we laughed until we cried that day, two girlfriends together in crisis, still being girls.

She had her breasts reconstructed from tissue on her stomach, terrible surgery but worth it, she said. She was always joking about her boobs growling when she got hungry. The only thing about them that she didn't like was that she didn't have any nipples. A few months ago she wrote me, and she was so excited. The doctor had created her some nipples, and she was about to go and have them tattooed. She did, and they turned out "Mary Kay Cadillac pink," so she went again to have them made a darker shade. We laughed and laughed over that. She finally got them the right color and was so happy to feel whole again. She was also overjoyed that she had a flat tummy again, as they had given her a tummy tuck to get the skin and tissue for her boobs. She was one sexy lady.

Patty and I liked all the same things and had the same wacky sense of humor. We went to see the movie *The Flintstones*. We loved the huge jewelry they were wearing in the movie, so we decided to make us some Flintstones jewelry. She got pieces of wood, and her husband, Morris, set her up with all the woodworking tools she needed. She made us these huge rings, some of which she stained, others she even painted leopard. I still wear those rings all the time! Then she decided she was going to go even further with her woodworking. She made me a life-size Betty Boop, complete with dog and fancy leash. Patty could do anything! She painted beautiful paintings, some of which I have hanging in our home.

She would send me boxes filled with the funniest things. I'd laugh until tears would stream down my face as I opened a plastic bag filled with white packing beads, which she had labeled "snowman poop." She made crazy things out of the stuff she had brought home from her many hospital stays. I never knew what to expect when I received a package or a card from Patty. But I knew I could expect a laugh.

One time I sent her a huge box of old jewelry. I knew she would turn it into something, and she did. She made huge rings for both of us out of one of the many pairs of earrings I'd sent. She glued the broken jewelry on everything from purses and shoes to towels. She just had a special knack for creating.

We had one rule when we went shopping together. We'd buy one matching outfit. Since we lived so far apart, it would remind us of each other every time we wore it, and the fun we'd had picking it out.

For Christmas this year she had some old 14K jewelry melted down, and she made us each a 14K gold toothpick. She knew I had had one for years and lost it.

She always told me she was my biggest fan. She had every record I'd ever made, every book I'd ever written, everything that had ever been written about me. She did an entire Tammy Faye bedroom, with all my memorabilia and pictures, pictures, pictures. Her one wish was that someday I'd come visit her house and stay in her Tammy Faye bedroom. I will feel sad the rest of my life that I never got to do that. I could not bear to walk into it now with her not there. It would break my heart into a million pieces. Yet somehow I think it would make her happy that I finally saw "my" room.

I cannot imagine how Morris is going to be able to walk back into their house. She brought such life and laughter to everything. How is he going to be able to deal with the quiet of the house? She was a presence bigger than life. He had built her a little house to put her tanning bed in. She was so proud of it. It was heated and air-conditioned. Her little getaway. She talked to me so many times about it. How does one ever deal with walking into her special place knowing she will never be there again? How can he possibly walk into her closet filled with her wonderful clothes, shoes, purses, jewelry, all the things that said, "I'm Patty! These are the things I love!"? How does one put away the perfume and lipstick, the bath oils and soaps, how does one wash the towels that contain her aroma? What about the bathrobe that hangs behind the bathroom door? What does one do with her purse filled with "Patty stuff"? Her wallet, credit cards, makeup, all the things a woman carries in her purse? When she left her house that day, she never knew she would not be coming home again.

She was not feeling well that day. The doctor had told her she was fine, it was nothing to worry about. But her bones ached and her head was hurting. Her sister was with her and said, "Patty, why don't we go over to the chiropractor? That'll make your neck feel better." She ran upstairs to get dressed. Her sister heard her scream her name and found Patty lying on the bed. She had suffered a stroke. The ambulance was called; they wheeled her out and she died in the hospital two weeks later. The sadness of that is overwhelming to me.

She loved animals. She had a dog, a little girl poodle she had named Tammy Faye. The dog lived to be really old. When Patty realized that Tammy Faye was dying, she put strawberry jelly on her finger, and little Tammy Faye died licking that jelly off Patty's finger. She replaced Tammy Faye with a little bulldog so ugly he's cute. Her Christmas card this year was a picture of that dog with a Santa Claus hat on his head. I know how much that little dog will miss "his mommy." He must have wondered what was happening as they placed her on the stretcher to take her away. I know he was running along behind and licking her hand until they closed the door and left him there alone.

What does one do with a little animal that loved its owner so much when that person is never coming back?

Patty and Morris have two boys. She loved them more than life itself. She was so proud of them. She was so looking forward to being a Grandmother. She couldn't wait. We'd talk about it.

I don't know if Patty knew she was dying or not. I don't think she did. She had beat weeks of chemotherapy in the hospital before. I feel sure she thought she'd be going back home again. This time it wasn't cancer. I wonder if the thought of dying ever passed through her mind. I hope not. They kept her so drugged and sedated the last few days I don't think she knew anything. She was sleeping all the time. I'd like to think that she went to sleep and just woke up in Heaven.

One day we will see each other again. That is the hope of a Christian. The hope helps us deal one day at a time with the tragedies of life. The terrible losses in life. The disappointments and the hurts of life. This world is not our home, we are just passing through. The sign on my mom's casket said, "Going Home." Patty went home today.

Girlfriend Stuff

The greatest blessing one can have is friends—close, long-time friends. People you know you can trust. I have been truly blessed with awesome girlfriends.

Why are girlfriends important to a woman?

Women understand women (from sweetness to cattiness).

Women understand petty things that men just don't get!

Women LOVE to talk, talk, talk (all of us).

We help in raising each other's kids.

We understand shopping—it's an exercise, *not* an addiction.

We have to help each other lose weight.

We understand the horrible *need* for chocolate once a month.

We understand the need to "do lunch."

We love bargains and understand the need to be first in line, even if we have to be there for hours ahead of time.

We all hide clothes in our car until we can sneak them into the house when our husbands aren't looking.

We love shoes! (We agree a girl can *never* have too many shoes!)

We love jewelry! (Or have too much jewelry.)

We can literally "shop till we drop." It's not just a saying!

We can cry together (actually cry real tears). *(continued)*

Girlfriend Stuff *(cont'd)*

We can laugh till we wet our pants—then laugh at that!

We can give each other advice.

We love "girl meetings" *if* the men can be there too.

We critique each other through eyes of love (most of the time).

We trade clothes . . . according to our weight at the time.

We can cry together over sad movies.

We can create all kinds of things.

We like makeup.

We like perfume and bubble bath and candlelight.

We hate housework. At least I do! So do all my friends.

We can spend the night at each other's homes and not feel like we are intruding—after all, we're family!

We encourage each other.

We tell the truth about how you *really* look in this bathing suit.

We say, "Oh, honey, you're not fat, you're just curvy, and that's sexy."

We share birth control secrets.

We go to the hospital together. (One goes, we all go!)

We give each other gifts for no reason.

We send each other cards for no reason.

We can disagree and still be friends.

We can become little girls again at the drop of a hat.

We take care of each other's pets.

We treat our pets like children—we even put little coats on them in the cold.

We cut and color each other's hair.

We share magazines and magazine articles.

We share secrets till the day we die that never go any further than between us.

We pray for each other.

We have plastic surgery together—a little nip here, a tuck there!

We talk about getting older and share what's falling where.

We are grandmothers together.

We understand when one of us fails and do not condemn each other.

We realize that we are not perfect but love each other anyway.

We share lipstick.

We eat off each other's plates.

We share desserts.

We travel together.

We play jokes on each other.

We share quick recipes.

If a pet has to be put to sleep and you can't face it, your girlfriend will take it for you, then comfort you afterward.

Your girlfriends will help you face things you cannot face alone.

And no matter how far apart you are geographically, when you get back together you just take up where you left off, as if you were never apart.

10.

Roe and Me at Home

I have an awesome husband. He is always so put-together. I have never seen Roe Messner look bad! And he also smells good. Before he climbs into bed at night, I can smell his Chanel for men. On the other hand, at home you will generally find me in my old pink, hair-color-stained bathrobe. I never go out of the house unless I am dressed well, so at home I can be that little gal from International Falls. Little or no makeup, bare feet, and my short hair all askew. That's me at home.

When I get ready for the day I doll all up, no matter where I am going or what I am going to do that day. I hate to disappoint people. They expect a certain look and I *never* fail them. But the very first thing I do when I get back home is run for that old pink bathrobe.

If we don't go out for dinner, it's soup for Roe and cereal for me. If I'm really hungry, I'll add a bagel. Roe watches sports on

TV while I busy myself with whatever. At night I belong to my two little dogs, Tuppins (a three-pound Yorkie) and Muffie (an eight-pound poodle combination). They won't let me out of their sight. They get up on my bed with me and we snuggle until Daddy comes into the bedroom. Muffie puts on a ferocious act of growling and Tuppins chimes in, barking. I have to rescue Roe from the little monsters. It's a merry chase! They sleep in our large bathroom in their doggie beds.

The TV is mine at night—no sports allowed in our bedroom! That's Roe's choice. He goes to sleep long before I do. I'm a night owl! I keep "goodies" like jelly beans, cookies, and banana circus peanuts stored in our TV cabinet. Roe says that's where the "good stuff" is. He says I'm like a little mouse scurrying around in the middle of the night.

I have finally figured out why Roe goes right to sleep. It's my Vicks! My mom said that Vicks heals everything. When we were kids, she stuffed it up our noses, rubbed it on our chests, made us swallow it when we had sore throats. I remember one time my brother had an awful earache. I was baby-sitting all the kids, so I told him not to worry, I'd make him feel better. So what did I do? I went and got the Vicks bottle. I got a teaspoon and melted some over the stove, then poured it into my brother's aching ear. My mom could have killed me. The poor kid couldn't hear for a week—the Vicks had hardened in his ear. But I think his earache went away.

Well, anyway, that's where I got my love of Vicks. Now I put Vicks on my throat at night simply because it comforts me. It makes me think of Mom, I guess. And guess what—at my age I still don't have one wrinkle on my neck! It has to be the Vicks. Roe laughs at me and shakes his head.

When the sandman finally hits me, I cuddle up in my old, ratty, long gown—pink, of course; has to match the bathrobe—and thank God that I am lying next to the man I love. And that he loves me in spite of my funny antics.

Oh, I'm putting Vicks in my nose tonight, too. It clears the head. . . . I think!

11.
Little Things Mean a Lot

I often feel sorry for men trying to please the women in their life. They can be a little clumsy about it, like a fat little puppy learning how to walk. We women can be hard to figure out; most of the time *we* don't even know what we want, so how can we expect them to know?

So I have written down the things that make me feel loved:

✳ When he says, "Honey, do we need to talk?" (Wow, he noticed!) I love it when my husband takes time to just talk to me.

✳ When he gives up something he loves doing (golf) to do something I want to do.

✳ When he doesn't seem to notice that the credit card is a little over the top this month!

✳ When he does the grocery shopping. (This really makes me feel he loves me.)

✳ Today he scrubbed the kitchen floor.

✳ When he tells me he loves me during the day.

✳ When he allows me to help my kids financially.

✳ I love the fact that he loves just the two of us being together. (He doesn't always want to have another couple with us.)

✳ When we plan "dates." That's fun!

✳ I love how he goes to so much trouble to pick out cards for special occasions. And the fact that he shops for a gift—he *hates* shopping!

✳ When he fixes things around the house.

✳ When he puts gas in my car.

✳ I love the fact that when I have to travel, he insists on going with me. I feel loved and safe.

✳ I love the fact that the first thing I see each morning when I walk into our kitchen is my husband sitting at the table reading his Bible.

✳ I love how he worries about me when he has to be out of town for a few days.

✳ He always encourages me. He seems proud of me. That makes me do a better job.

✳ He takes care of the checkbook, paying the bills, etc. That makes me feel loved. He tells me, "Honey, you don't have to work. I can take care of you."

✳ The other day when I was having a "royal fit," he put his arms around me and said, "Honey, you just need a hug." Even though I pulled away, it gave me a warm, fuzzy feeling inside.

✳ I love it that when I'm upset and screaming, "Just leave me alone!" he knows that's when I need his love and understanding the most.

✳ And I *love* the fact that he loves my makeup!

Little Things
Mean a Lot

Now I want you to make your list of the things that make you feel loved. When you're done, leave it lying around where your loved one can see it!

1. _____
2. _____
3. _____
4. _____
5. _____
6. _____
7. _____
8. _____
9. _____
10. _____
11. _____
12. _____
13. _____
14. _____
15. _____
16. _____
17. _____
18. _____
19. _____
20. _____

12.

The
Peeing
Contest

My two grandsons, James and Jonathan, and their friend David were getting bored swimming in our pool in the backyard. So they asked me if they could take the dogs for a walk. I said yes and put the collars and leashes on Tuppins, Muffin, and their little eight-pound pompoo Jay Cee, and the three boys and three dogs were on their way.

About a half hour later, just as Grandma here had started to worry, I heard barking and lots of laughter. They came running in the front door, laughing so hard they could hardly stand.

"Grandma, we had a peeing contest! We decided that whichever dog peed the most would be the winner. Muffin peed twenty-seven times and Tuppins peed seventeen times and Jay Cee only peed twelve times."

"So who had Muffin?" I asked. A proud James stepped up

and took a bow. Just then, Muffin decided he had one more pee left in him for the bottom of the stairs. As I went to get the Clorox Clean-Up, I thought how wonderful and fun little boys are. They can make a contest out of anything. I'm so glad I'm their grandma.

———

One night my daughter and grandsons were visiting me while Roe was out of town. Just as they were to leave for home, a horrendous storm blew in. It was late and every light in the house went out, plunging us into total darkness and silence. No TVs blaring, no computer humming, no air conditioner whirring. We all reached out for each other in the darkness and began to search for candles. At first we were all scared to death, then a strange excitement took hold of us. We were laughing and bumping into one another, looking in all the drawers for matches, looking for the lantern or a stray flashlight we'd bought for that exact purpose. We finally found the matches and lit the candles, which led us to the lantern. We all crept up the stairs to my bedroom and dove onto my big, soft feather bed. I will never forget that night, the four of us and the two little dogs all cuddling together in that big bed, the room lit only by candlelight, and stillness that you could cut with a knife.

At first we didn't know what to do without TV to watch and video games to play—until we started to talk. We told family stories and laughed until we cried. We hugged each other and watched the candlelight make strange shadows on the wall and the ceiling. And we wished with all our hearts that the lights wouldn't come back on that night. We all fell asleep on the bed in the middle of conversations, smiles on our faces.

When we awoke, every light and every TV in the house was

on and life was back to normal again. But we still talk about that being one of the best nights we ever had. The four of us and two dogs. Tammy Faye, Tammy Sue, James and Jonathan, Muffie and Tuppie.

We never found that flashlight.

My Favorite Recipes

Dump Cake

1 (20-oz.) can crushed pineapple
1 (21-oz.) can cherry pie filling (or any fruit you might
* like, such as peaches, etc.)*
1 box white cake mix
butter
walnuts for garnish
ice cream or Cool Whip

Pour pineapple and cherry pie filling into a 12 × 8 oblong pan. The fruit should cover the entire bottom of the pan. Pour white cake mix (right from the box) over the top. Dot with butter and walnuts. Bake for about 25 to 30 minutes at 350 degrees until it is brown and bubbly.

Top with ice cream or Cool Whip. Delicious!

Fudge

3 cups sugar
1½ sticks butter (3/4 cup)
milk (enough to just moisten ingredients)
1 bag chocolate chips
1 jar marshmallow cream
dash of vanilla extract
walnuts (optional)

In a medium-sized saucepan over low heat, heat sugar, butter, and milk until butter is melted and sugar is dissolved, 3 to 4 minutes. Then add:

1 jar marshmallow cream

vanilla extract

walnuts (if using)

Stir together with wooden spoon and spread in nonstick cookie sheet. I usually dive right in at this point (ha!), but you really should let it set for about 10 minutes. Then cut it up and enjoy.

(continued)

My Favorite Recipes *(cont'd)*

Crockpot Chicken

chicken. Wash the chicken first!
salt and pepper
*1 to 2 cans of condensed cream of chicken soup**
chopped celery (about 1/2 cup)
4 large potatoes cut in half (or more to taste)
5 carrots (or more to taste)
2 large onions

Place chicken in crockpot. Salt and pepper to taste. Cover with cream of chicken soup.

Add chopped celery, potatoes, carrots, and onions. Allow it to simmer all day (5 to 6 hours will do), but if you're going to be gone for more than eight hours, I'd put the crockpot on low.

Get home from a hard day's work and you have a wonderful, nutritious dinner ready to eat!

*For instance, for a 3- to 4-pound chicken, you'll need 2 cans of soup.

Chili

1 pound hamburger meat
1 medium-sized onion peeled and chopped
salt and pepper
1 (28-oz.) can tomatoes
1 (26-oz.) can kidney beans
chili powder to taste

Place hamburger meat, onion, and salt and pepper in a medium-sized skillet. Brown the beef. Then add tomatoes, kidney beans, and chili pepper to taste.

Simmer for about one hour. (If you're really hungry, 15 to 20 minutes.)

Pizza

4 to 6 flour tortillas
spaghetti sauce (to cover tortillas)
meat of choice (we like cooked hamburger)
vegetables of choice (we like green peppers, onions,
  olives)
mozzarella cheese, shredded

Cover a pizza pan with four tortillas. Spread spaghetti sauce, meat of choice, and vegetables of choice evenly over tortillas. Top with cheese. Bake at 400 degrees until cheese is melted and pizza is a bit crispy.

(continued)

My Favorite Recipes *(cont'd)*

Cream Peas on Toast (my kids' favorite)

1 stick butter (1/2 cup), melted
flour
milk
salt (a pinch)
1 cup canned peas
toast

Melt stick of butter in saucepan. Mix flour and milk gradually in a large glass bowl. Add a pinch of salt. Shake or stir or do both until it is free of lumps. Slowly add flour and milk mixture, stirring constantly to avoid lumps. Add peas. Continue to stir over medium heat until thick and bubbly. (If too thick, add more milk; if too thin, add more flour, stirring constantly.)

Serve over toast and enjoy.

Rice Dessert

rice (enough for as many people as you're feeding.
   See box for serving size.)
1 (20-oz.) can crushed pineapple
1 (8-oz.) tub Cool Whip
tiny marshmallows (optional)

Cook rice per directions, drain very well, and cool. In a large bowl, combine rice, pineapple, Cool Whip, and tiny marshmallows, and serve.

Delicious!

13.

Little Things Mean a Lot, Part II

My husband and I no longer have any children at home. However, that does not mean that we do not miss our kids. I moved back to Charlotte just to be near my daughter and grandsons and my son and his wife.

I think that sometimes when our kids leave home we miss them so much—they have been a part of our lives for so long— that we have unrealistic expectations of them. We still feel a certain amount of control over their lives, which they end up resenting. And we can't figure out why. We only want to help. But kids, when they move away from home, want to do it their way. They want to try their wings. And we must allow them to, even if they keep crashing to the ground. They'll eventually find their way. It takes some longer than others, but that's okay.

What is it that the kids do that makes me happy? Okay, Sissy and Jamie, here goes:

❋ I love it when you stop by for a visit.

❋ I love it when you call me.

❋ I love it when I call you and you don't hang up saying, "Mom, I've got a lot to do today, I can't talk."

❋ I love the fact that when I had to go into the hospital, you were there with me every day, and I had not even asked you to be there. (My daughter flew all the way to California when she heard I had cancer, and she took care of me night and day until I was well. That is the greatest show of love a child can give a parent.)

❋ I love knowing that we will be together on holidays.

❋ I love the fact that my daughter wants her children to spend time with me.

❋ I love it when we can sometimes go shopping together. She and her girlfriend came and kidnapped me one day. We ate out and spent the whole day shopping. She will never know how much that meant to me.

If I could sum up what I as a parent love, it's just occasionally being able to spend time—time, time, that's the magic word!—with the people I love more than anything in the world. Tammy Sue Bakker, James Chapman, Jonathan Chapman, Jamie Charles Bakker, and Amanda Bakker.

And I think the hardest thing about having grown children is that when they walk out your door you know they are in no way obligated to walk back in. Coming home, to me, says, "Mom, I love you." Jamie and Amanda come and spend a few days with me every few months. That means the world to me. I get the chance to talk to them, cook for them, shop with them, and just be family again. My kids love Roe, and Roe loves my kids. He loves his own kids and grandkids and often takes trips back to Wichita, Kansas, just to see his kids play ball and wrestle. I feel we have a wonderful relationship with all our "blended" children and grandchildren. He has fifteen grand-children and four children. I have two children and two grand-children.

To Moms and Dads:

WARNING! Don't try to run your children's lives once they leave home. They will resent you for it! Remember when you left home as a young person. You felt so grown-up and capa-ble. Well, they feel the same way. They must be allowed to live their own lives, make their own mistakes, and raise their own children. We as parents just need to let them know that we still love them and are there if they need us.

And this:

Parents, live your own lives! Do the things you have always wanted to do. And spend the kids' inheritance! Ha! You earned it! Enjoy it!

14.

A Man Named Joe

He came as a great surprise into my life. An old-fashioned, yet up-to-date, 100 percent pure southern gentleman—the kind you read about in stories of the South. They live on big plantations, have servants, and rich, soft southern accents.

I don't know why this man decided he needed to find Tammy Faye. I had never done anything for him, had never given him anything, had never had him on television with me, and he had never even been to my home. He didn't know any of my friends. I cannot imagine how in the world he found me.

So many people who were a great part of my life—that I had on TV with me, that I had given many things to, that I had done many things for, and who have been to my home many times— said they weren't with me when I needed them most because they couldn't find me. But when I hear them say that I know in my heart that they could not find me because they didn't bother to look. Or didn't care enough to look. When they say that to me, I just nod and smile, but my heart knows . . .

I was living in Palm Springs, California. I attended Victory Christian Center every Sunday. I shopped and ate out. I certainly wasn't hiding from anybody. My friends could have located me very easily. My divorce from Jim and my move to California was widely publicized. Who didn't know where I was? Yet no one could find me.

Except Joe! He called the church I attended and, through our pastor, who gave us his number, arranged to come all the way from Colorado to have lunch with Roe and me. Joe not only found me; he flew across the country to see and talk to me. God bless Joe!

He came as a man with a mission. "Tammy, you need to get back to the people again," he told me. "They miss you."

That was news to me! I had been lonely and hurting for so long. Only my closest girlfriends seemed to care. And now this man is telling me that people miss me? Joe said to me, "You need to sing again. You need to start doing things again."

I don't really know how I felt when he said that. Maybe he was misinformed. I had once been a part of the largest Christian television network in the world. I was on TV every day, sold millions of books. But that was yesterday. Today I was forgotten and alone. What did this man know about people wanting to hear me again?

A great sadness overwhelmed me, but at the same time I felt a small ray of hope that maybe, just maybe, people still did care. Then a wave of fear washed over me. What if he was wrong? What if they didn't?

Joe was in the flea market business. He said, "Tammy, why don't you come to one of my flea markets? You can sing, talk with the people, do local television and radio, and get your feet wet again." He said he would pay for my and Roe's airline tickets, put us up in a nice hotel, plus he would give me a paycheck when it was all over.

My heart was racing. It was too good to be true. Should I do it? Could I do it? Should I take the chance of being rejected again? We finished our lunch, shook hands with Joe, and left.

I couldn't wait to talk this over with Roe. My first question was, Was this what God wanted me to do? Flea markets??? It seemed too good to be true. You know how I love to shop!

Roe was adamant. "Honey, I think this is a good thing, and I think we should do it." I trusted his judgment, and when Joe contacted us the next day, we booked the event. I never dreamed that God was going to use a wonderful man named Joe to open up my life again. A man who told me he watched me on TV for years, that he could not believe I was not doing anything, and that his goal in life was to put me back where I belonged—back with the people!

It has been many years since that lunch in Palm Springs. Joe Spotts and I are still together. My life has turned from a tightly closed bud to a full blooming flower. I have done things and been places and seen things that few people get to experience. Joe's belief in me as a person, as a TV personality, as a singer, and as a speaker has changed my life. And with Joe's support, along with my husband's—who backs me up 100 percent and believes in me as much as Joe does—I am now preaching, singing, doing TV and radio, doing a one-woman show all over the country, have had television documentaries done on my life, and I am again writing a book.

Joe has never taken a dime from me or from Roe. He said, "Tammy Faye, I'd rather be your friend. If I start charging you, it will change that." I have tried and tried to pay Joe. They say managers can charge up to 20 percent of everything you make. Not Joe! He gives of himself unselfishly so he can realize his dream of "Tammy being back out there with the people where she belongs." Thank you, Joe, for caring enough to "find me." And thank you for giving me the confidence that I needed so desperately. For giving me back the faith in myself that hurt and sadness and loneliness had taken away. I will always love you.

It's a
Bumpy
Ride,
So Hang On!

15.

Don't Be
a Victim

Refuse to be a victim of your circumstances. You can only become a victim if you *allow* yourself to become a victim.

I have had some unbelievable things happen in my life. Things I could not predict; things I could not stop. And once the bad things happened, they began to snowball, they just rolled down the hill faster and faster and got bigger and bigger, until I was nearly smothered to death in grief and hurt and anger and disappointment.

I don't like to go back and rehash things that have happened. There's one thing I have learned: You cannot go forward looking in the rearview mirror. And I've never been good at backing up! But if my going back there will help someone else, I will.

When I was a little girl helping my mom raise eight of us kids, I had one prayer. As I would ride my bicycle down the old road in International Falls, I would always pray: "Lord, *please* don't let my life be boring!" Well, I smile as I say, Be careful what you pray for, you just might get it. One thing my life has **not** been is boring.

I'll just hit a few highlights—or should I say lowlights—of my life so you know. But let's not dwell on them. . . .

My first real hurt that I remember was at seventeen. I was engaged to marry a wonderful young man and felt I had to break the engagement. I cried for weeks over that decision but felt it was the right thing to do.

The night I married Jim Bakker, we heard a knock on our apartment door. It was that young man, checking to make sure I was all right. I felt as if a bolt of lightning hit me right in the stomach when I saw him standing there. But at least I knew he really cared for me.

I was married to Jim for about a week when I found out something he had managed to keep hidden from me while we were dating. I always tell young people, When you marry someone, expect a surprise. You'll always find out something you didn't know when you start to live with another person. The surprise will either be a good surprise or a bad surprise. The surprise I had was that Jim had a terrible problem with depression. It was hard for me to understand depression at that time, as I had always been such a positive, happy person.

So, right from the start I learned about another side of life. And that was very hard on me. But I loved Jim, and my mission in life was to try and make him happy and keep him happy—to try and keep his depression at bay. It's very hard to try and help what you don't understand. But I did my best. Sometimes it worked, sometimes it didn't. And when it didn't work, I'd blame myself. I spent thirty years trying to help one of the most intelligent men I have ever met with a problem that I could not solve. I never thought less of him; I just felt terribly sorry for him. When I found out Jim had had a one-night stand with another woman, I wanted to die. It was the straw that broke the camel's back in our already troubled marriage. And finally I just got too tired to try anymore. I gave up. Whether that was right or wrong of me, I have to leave my decision with God. He knew my heart then and He knows it now. I didn't give up my marriage to be mean, but I may have given it up for a selfish reason—to save myself. When you want to be a wife but end up feeling like a mother instead, well . . .

I don't even like the sound of the word "divorce," and yet it happened to me. It was the lowest moment of my life, because I felt that I had failed. The day my divorce became final I felt as if I were totally and utterly alone, without a friend in the world. The ache in my heart was impossible to measure. Unless you've been there, there is no way of understanding that particular feeling of failure.

Jim and I built three huge ministries in our thirty years together. We helped Pat Robertson build the Christian Broadcasting Network. We left on our own accord after nine years of working with Pat. We started and built up the Trinity Broadcasting Network. It was a huge success, but we were voted out by a new board of directors put together by the people we were working with. Then we started the PTL network. It was an exhilarating time. We built the largest Christian network in the world, including Heritage USA. The last year we were there, six million people visited Heritage USA. It was the third most-visited place in the United States, third only to Disneyland and Disney World.

We lost PTL and Heritage USA because another minister revealed Jim's one-night stand to the news media and they saw an opportunity for a huge story and ran with it. As hard as we tried, we did not have the money to fight the case against us. The lies had somehow become truth in people's minds. We had been on live TV for twenty-five years; we loved the people and they loved us. We never tried to hide anything from them—we lived our lives in front of the cameras. The good and the bad of our lives. We would *never* have done anything to hurt those people. The saddest moment of my life was to have our integrity questioned and then destroyed by another minister of the Gospel.

> Other people can stop you temporarily; only *you* can stop you permanently.

Besides being extremely intelligent, Jim Bakker has another wonderful quality. He was and is an honest man. To be accused of dishonesty nearly destroyed me. And it nearly destroyed Jim. I don't think he will ever fully recover from what happened to him, to the partners of PTL, and to our family. I don't even try to defend Jim or myself anymore. Those who loved PTL know the truth and don't need proof. Those who don't, well, they don't matter to me anymore. God knows what really happened, and that's all that's important.

Jim was sent to prison as a result of what happened. He was paraded across the TV screens of America, chained like an animal. Twenty years later they still run that footage. And they still laugh and make fun of Jim's horrible suffering. At Jim's trial, Judge Potter actually covered his ears, yawned, winked at the jury, and denied evidence that could have helped Jim. When he was questioned by our lawyers as to why he would not allow that evidence, he just laughed and said you can take it up on appeal.

Jim was given a sentence of *forty-five years* in prison. Some murderers don't even receive that kind of sentence. He ended up serving only five years, because his lawyers believed he was innocent and helped him.

When you have three thousand people working for you and you're responsible for decisions they make, there will be mistakes. We never claimed to be perfect. Yes, we made mistakes, but they were not *criminal* mistakes! Thank God all the other Christian organizations learned from our mistakes and have profited greatly as a result.

Then there was Roe. Roc Messner built Heritage USA, our huge resort for the people who visited us. It was several miles square. Buses and trams and little trains carried people to their destinations on the grounds. Women shopped at the beautiful stores, men fished in the lakes, children played at one of the biggest waterslides in the country. Everyone rode the beautiful merry-go-round. People prayed in an exact replica of the Upper Room in Israel. They filled a giant amphitheater to watch talented players re-create the life of Jesus. They ate in some of the finest restaurants in the country.

A thousand people a day crowded into the huge TV studio, where we shot live programming every day. They filled the huge Barn Auditorium, where we had church services on Sunday. We had conferences, banquets, plays, and church services that went on every day. In the afternoon, those who wanted to could be in the audience for *Tammy's House Party*, televised Monday through Friday.

There was a place for everyone at Heritage USA. We had beautiful quarters where street people could stay, learn a trade, and get their lives back together again. We had a beautiful facility on the grounds for unwed mothers who had chosen not to abort their babies. We gave them jobs at PTL and got their babies adopted by Christian homes. So many little ones were saved as a result of The Girls' Home. We had marriage seminars and financial seminars; something was available at all times to help people. We had a grade school (1–12), and a college to train young people in television. Today, people trained at Heritage are working all over the world. We had a place called Kevin's House, where we took care of kids who had to be institutionalized because of terminal illnesses. It was a wonderful place, with a petting zoo and horses close by. Those who stayed there loved it so. We gave so many children a chance to find some happiness at the end of their short lives.

PTL provided airplanes for missionaries, hospitals for India, and medical equipment. We also had a prison ministry through which inmates had access to twenty-four-hour-a-day Christian television programs. We provided Bibles by the hundreds of thousands to prisons, missionaries, and anyone else who needed one. We also had thousands of places all over the United States where we fed and clothed people. They were called People That Love Centers.

At Heritage, Roe built some of the most beautiful hotels you have ever seen. Hundreds of people also lived right there on the grounds in the homes we built.

Roe was known by everyone at Heritage USA. He was a church-builder—he's built over sixteen hundred of our nation's churches. His reputation was one of honesty. Jim and Roe worked closely together building hundreds of buildings. That's how I met Roe and came to know that he was a man who could be trusted, a good man. Some people accuse Roe and me of getting together at PTL, but that was not the case at all. I hardly ever saw him; he was always building, and I was always doing TV and everything else associated with it. I can remember Roe coming out to our home one time. We were eating supper when he arrived, and we invited him to join us. That's the only time I ever actually remember talking to him at Heritage. He said I was stuck up and would never speak to him, but that isn't so. He was never anywhere where I could speak to him.

You never know where the twists and turns of life will lead you. We can get lost so easily when we lose sight of the One who knows the way—God. I know there are times I've lost my way, times I ran away and hid from God like a rebellious little kid. Times when I thought I knew the way better than He did. Then I'd get ahead of His plan for me, only to find out that I had to wait for Him anyway. I've learned so much through the years of my life. Lessons I would so love to teach the younger generations. What's important in life, and what isn't.

> When your dreams turn to dust, vacuum!

Many people say that Jim and I were victims of a cruel society, a cruel judge, a cruel preacher, and a sometimes not-so-fair justice system. I have never felt that way. I believe you can only become a victim if you allow yourself to become a victim. Some people have a victim mentality. It may be the way they're raised, or it may just be their personality.

What happened to you happened. But that's yesterday, and yesterday is gone. Today is what we have right now. We should not spoil today by worrying about tomorrow either. Tomorrow may never come. So I give today everything I can give it. I try to make today count.

Think of Princess Di. I know she never in her wildest dreams thought that night when she got in the car with her friend that she would never see tomorrow. I'm sure she thought she had years yet to live. JFK Jr. and his beautiful wife and her sister were just going to a wedding. They'd be home by the next day, back in their Manhattan apartment; their dog would be coming to the door to greet them as usual. But that didn't happen. We never know what tomorrow may bring. We must keep our hearts right with each other, and with God.

I never dreamed that I would have a *second* husband sent to prison. It was unthinkable. But it happened. Roe went to prison after having to file for bankruptcy. He lost $18 million when PTL went down. They tried to indict Roe along with Jim but couldn't. All Roe did was build Heritage. But Roe's ex-wife and her divorce lawyer turned him in to the DA, saying he had not declared all his assets when he filed for bankruptcy. The court believed her and her lawyer. Roe went to prison for two years over $20,000. Then, before they would allow us to leave the state of California, where Roe was imprisoned, they made him pay back the $20,000 they said he owed. To whom, we don't know. The DA who put Roe in prison subsequently resigned and ran for Congress. Roe was his last case!

I came close to becoming a victim of my own emotions when that happened. They talk about the straw that broke the camel's back. Well, that was almost it for me. I was all alone for the first time in my life. I had no one. My mom had died, my children were thousands of miles away, all that was left were me and my dogs.

But I had God! I was not going to let those who'd set out to destroy us win. The God I serve is bigger than any destruction the devil can bring against us. "Greater is He that is in us than he that is in the world." That is God's promise. He has also promised us that when we go through "deep waters they shall not overflow us." That He will bring us safely to the other side.

For two long years I drove one hundred miles every weekend to visit my husband in prison. My heart ached every day. I was lonely and scared, but I grabbed hold of those promises mentally. Romans 8:28 became my rock that steadied me. "For we know that all things work together for good to those that love the Lord and to those that are the called according to his purpose." I knew the God I served would not let me down. And He didn't!

16.

Pain

I have been through much pain in my life. And I often think of what would have happened to me had I allowed pain to dominate my life, as it well could have. I would either be a very mean, angry, discouraged woman . . . or I would be dead by now.

I am talking about mental pain, not physical pain. There is a great difference between the two. Physical pain can generally be stopped, or at least lessened, by medications and healing drugs. Mental pain cannot be controlled by medication, drugs, alcohol, or the like. You may think you can control your mental pain through these things, but it's like putting a Band-Aid on the problem. You just cover it up for a while. One day the infection deep within is going to have to be dealt with, is going to have to be let out.

Some of us cause our own mental pain because we dwell on the sadness, the unfairness, the cruelty of what we have gone through. Our mind is like a cow chewing her cud, chewing it over and over and over and over. We can't just chew it once and swallow it and allow nature to take its course. We dwell on it and dwell on it and dwell on it, over and over and over. Why did that person have to die? Why did I lose my job? Why don't I have more money? Why don't I have any friends? Why did he or she do that to me? Why am I sick? Why am I being picked on? Why do *they* get all the breaks? Why, why, why, why?

There are so many questions that have no answers. And all the whys in the world will never be able to satisfy your longing to know. We should not waste precious time on those questions. We need to leave them in the hands of an all-knowing God, who *never* makes a mistake when it comes to His children. Only God knows the answers to all of our questions.

This is something I must practice continually. I try not to dwell on the questions. Why did my brother Donny die? Why did my sister Judy die of cancer? Why did my mom die so young? Why did we work our entire life to build the world's largest TV ministry and then lose it all? Why did God allow people to hurt our family so bad? Why did two husbands go to prison? Why did I get colon cancer?

The answers to all those I have to leave with God. To me, there are no answers. Oh, maybe some of you think you could answer them for me, but you couldn't. No one could. Not the greatest psychologist or psychiatrist or doctor. Only the God I serve knows the answers, and He doesn't have to tell me why. I think it's part of truly trusting God. It's the faith that can let go. And without faith, the Bible says it's impossible to please God. I want my life to be pleasing to God.

Be careful what you rent space in your mind to. You can't stop the whys from flying over your mind, but you don't need to allow them to lodge there! Ask God to cover your mind with the blood of Jesus every day. I do that. The blood that Jesus shed on Calvary is still as powerful today as it was in the Bible. We can claim that precious blood that was spilled on Calvary for you and for me. I believe one of the biggest mistakes we as Christians make today is that we no longer want to hear about the blood. We have taken it out of our songbooks: Ministers no longer preach about the blood—it's not the popular thing to do these days. But it is a trick of the devil to take away from us the power we have through the blood of Jesus.

> For those who believe in God, no explanation is necessary. For those who don't, no explanation is possible.

Did you every think that maybe, just maybe, God allows things to take place in our lives—uncomfortable, hurtful things at the time—because He and He alone can see the Big Picture? We only see the small picture, what is happening now. God sees the Big Picture—our future. And the things He has in mind for us are not for evil but for good.

Think about Job. God himself alerted the devil to Job: "Have you seen my servant Job?" He told the devil he could do anything he wanted to Job except kill him. The Bible says Job was a good man, so we know it was not because of sin in his life that God allowed Job to be tried. I get tired of hearing people say, "Oh, he must have had some sin in his life—that's why he's having so much trouble." Job had no sin in his life when the devil was trying to destroy him by taking his family and all his worldly possessions, leaving him sitting in an ash pile, taunting him. How discouraged Job must have become over the inhumanity of people who were supposed to be his friends. His own wife even said, "Job, why don't you just curse God and die?" But God knew the Big Picture. He knew what was in store for Job if he stayed faithful to Him. I'm sure at the time

Job must have thought it was all over for him. But his trust in God was greater than his need for human comforts or human confirmation of him as a person. He said, "Though God slay me, yet will I trust Him." What great faith we see in Job. What great *trust*.

We all know how the Big Picture played out. I believe Job could have chosen to die. But he chose to believe God and live. God restored his wealth and happiness to twice as much as before. Job 42:16 tells us Job lived 140 years after God restored everything. The story of Job has always brought me great hope and great comfort. When I need encouragement, I go back and read it again and again.

There's always someone who has it worse than you do. So many times I will hear about a family losing a child, or see someone who has lost their limbs, or a person who has become paralyzed and will forever have to have someone else take care of them, right down to taking them to the bathroom, brushing their teeth, turning them over in bed at night several times so that they can breathe. And I think, I don't have any problems at all. I am healthy, I can walk, I can talk, I can see, I can hear, I can take care of myself, my children are healthy, my grandchildren are healthy, I have a wonderful husband, I have a home, a car, I am warm in the cold winter and cool in the hot summer, I have food, and most of all I have God. I am, of all people, most blessed!

God help us to count our blessings. God help us to quit complaining. God help us to be thankful. I am so thankful I live in the United States of America. I could have been born in one of the Third World countries, but I was fortunate enough to be born in the USA.

When you're tempted to think about negative things, replace

those negative thoughts by counting your blessings. I want to be so filled with faith that there is no room in me for doubt and negativity. Fill me up, Lord, is my prayer. Fill me up with faith, with peace, with joy, so there can be no room for anything else in my mind, in my heart, in my being.

We need to quit feeling sorry for ourselves. And I'm preaching to myself. Quit having "pity parties." We need to begin to praise the Lord every day. We need to begin to thank the Lord every day. And we need to begin to trust the Lord every day. Trust Him in spite of circumstances, knowing that He does all things well and doesn't make any mistakes.

Pain can wrap itself around you like duct tape and squeeze the very life out of you if you allow it to. Grief is normal, but it will not bring a loved one back to life—it will not restore anything. We cannot let grief control our lives. Cry when you need to, but do not forget to smile too. The Bible says, "The joy of the Lord is our strength." When you lose your joy, you lose your strength, and that is when the devil can come in and torment you. It's fine to be sad over things that have happened in our lives. And we *need* to cry. I have shed so many tears. The sadness over deaths of people I love will always be there—but I will not allow sadness to control my life. And that is *my choice.* The sadness of losing Heritage USA will always be there. But I refuse to allow it to control my life. And that is my choice. *"Choose yea this day,"* the Bible says. *"Choose yea this day whom you will serve . . ."* The choice is ours. God has given us the power of choice.

Don't allow Satan to cloud your mind so you're incapable of making the right choices. He will cloud your mind with drugs, alcohol, discouragement, unbelief; he will use other people to cloud your mind. Don't let these things determine the choices you make. Ask God to help you, then listen, hear, and trust. So many people run to prophets for a word from the Lord. I am not putting down the value of God's prophets, but if God can speak to a prophet about your situation, then He can surely speak to you about it. And I'd rather hear it direct! You can hear from the same God Billy Graham serves, Oral Roberts serves, Mother Teresa served. God loves you just as much as He loves the great men and women of God that have made a name for themselves. You are no less important than they are in God's eyes.

17.

Facing Grief

Is there a right and a wrong way to grieve when you lose someone or something dear to you? I don't think so. I think facing grief is a very individual process. Some face it in silence, some scream and cry. Either way, you must get through it *your* way.

Patty Sewell was one of my best friends in the whole world. Patty and I shared a sister-type friendship. There wasn't anything I couldn't share with her, and no matter how awful it was, we would manage to laugh over it. We brought out the best in each other. We were always laughing and doing crazy things. She was such a joy to my life.

When I heard she had died, I could not believe it. I had just talked to her a few days before in the hospital and she sounded fine. She asked me when I was coming to see her, and when I told her I loved her, she said, "I love you more." Those were the last words I ever heard from my precious friend. We'd never laugh together again, we'd never make jewelry together again, we'd never shop together again, we'd never pull tricks on each other again, I'd never get another funny card from her. I'd never get another empty lipstick tube filled with Prevacid (an ulcer medicine she got cheaper than I could). She'd take the lipstick out of the tube and put the pills in. One time she sent me a white cake mix and told me on the phone to open it from the bottom. You could not tell it had ever been opened. I did as she said—more Prevacid!

We had such fun. I still cannot believe we'll never do those things again.

So how do I cope? How do I face the terrible loss of such a good friend? Well, you do what you have to do. You do what works for you. There is no right or wrong way to grieve.

The day after Patty died I took her out to eat and shop with me. Well, I took her picture, a framed picture she had signed for me. I talked to her. I didn't care what people thought. I just knew that she knew I was doing this. I felt her presence all day long. I cried and I cried and I cried some more. I spoke to my husband nonstop about the last time I talked to her. It helped me to talk about her. I called her sister and talked to her. I called her husband and talked to him. I talked to everyone in my house.

I have her picture sitting by an open Bible on a table in my house. Today it has a fresh rose by it. She would love that. I talk out loud to Patty as if she's still here. I feel that if indeed the Christians who have gone before us surround us in "so great a cloud of witness," then she can hear me talking to her.

I still cry whenever I talk about Patty. I will always miss her. Every time I open a drawer and see something she sent me, every time I wear one of the huge rings she made for me, every time I look at her picture smiling back at me, I will feel sadness that this vital, funny, fun, creative, smart lady is no longer with us. She died too young. Patty was just fifty-six years old. Sometimes I feel guilty that I am still alive and she is dead. And I ask God why He took her . . .

When my brother died suddenly I felt such grief I could hardly breathe. He was just fifty-seven. Gone in a second while walking his dog and laughing with his wife. The saddest day of my life was seeing him being carried into our little Assembly of God church in International Falls. He was going to be cremated. Cremation was the way his wife would cope with his death. She could take him back home. She could talk to his remains. That's fine. I think that would help me also. Even though I know that his spirit is with Jesus, at least some of what I knew (that precious body he lived in) is still here. It's funny, but it comforts me knowing that Donny is still with the woman he so loved. He would have liked that. I asked her to send me one of his shirts. She did and I put it on and wore it for days, hugging it to me, smelling his scent, talking to him as if he were there. I will miss my brother always.

When Mom died, I wanted to die too. I stood by her grave in the cold and rain, sobbing my heart out. I wished I were dead too, and that they could bury me next to her.

My sister sent me some of Mom's things—her nightgown, her rings, her perfume bottles (Estée Lauder), her diary, her glasses. I hung her nightgown next to mine for several weeks, holding on to it, crying until I could cry no more, reading her diary over and over and over again. I found out something so funny: She loved to vacuum. Every day she'd write, *I vacuumed today*. I still, several years later, cry over Mom. I miss her so much. I still find myself on special days—Christmas, Easter, Valentine's Day—wanting to call Mom or send Mom something. When something important happens in my life, my first instinct is always to call Mom. But Mom isn't there. Yes, I still talk to her pictures all over our house. "Hi, Mom! I miss you. I love you." I do what I have to do. It's my way of coping. My way of living without that person in my life. I also find that writing helps me.

I have had so many losses in my life. If I hadn't learned how to cope, I, too, would be dead. The loss of Heritage USA was a terrible loss to me. Heritage was the result of our life's work. Thirty years of hard work. It was all I knew, and suddenly it was gone. We were no longer allowed even to walk on the hundreds of acres of property we had lovingly developed. Our family's whole life was wrapped up in the work for the Lord we did at Heritage USA. It's all my daughter knew, it was all my son knew. It was their home, their school, their church, their playground, and all their friends were at Heritage USA. The first place of its kind visited by people from all over the world. *Gone!*

(The most horrible part of that was the way we lost it: through the unimaginable deceit and lies and plotting of people we thought were our friends. To understand the whole story, rent the documentary *The Eyes of Tammy Faye* at your local video store. Or read the book *Tammy: Telling It My Way*. It's a story that twenty years later people are still talking about and still do not fully understand.)

How did I deal with that loss? I had to do it my way. And even though many may not understand, it was the only way I knew to cope. I have been criticized, made fun of, ostracized by the church, told by people who were not there what I should have done and what I should not have done. But how do they know? They are not me, and they were not there.

I think your emotional makeup has a lot to do with the way

you have to grieve. Some people can accept the fact of loss and move on in life. I am an extremely sensitive person, and things that hurt cut deep into my very soul. I can never forget. So I must figure out how to live with the loss that hurts every day, some days more than others. I no longer cry over Heritage USA, but I will never get over the sadness of losing it. My son and my daughter are still learning how to deal with it. They still cry over it. They still hold on to their past, defending their parents, talking about how things used to be. The other day my daughter went back and visited the grounds of Heritage. Her grief was unimaginable, but she needed to go back and face what she had been avoiding for so many years. A ghost of the past, still standing there empty and lonely but still beautiful. Millions of dollars' worth of buildings, just sitting there decaying into the dust, rotting away.

I got a divorce from the man I had worked so hard with for thirty years. I did what the prayer says: *God grant me the serenity to accept the things I cannot change, the courage to change the things I can, and the wisdom to know the difference.* I know I cannot change what happened in the past. God has given me serenity and the wisdom to accept that fact. I have moved on in life. One day at a time I have gotten out of bed, faced the day ahead of me as a new day. And I have trusted God that Romans 8:28 still works: "For we know that all things work together for good to those that love God and to those that are the called according to His purpose."

I have never blamed God. I have always trusted God in spite of circumstances. The last time I walked through Heritage USA was during the filming of *The Eyes of Tammy Faye.* I could not face it alone. I took along my friend Judy Bycura. She and her husband, Blair, were our neighbors for many years. We raised our kids together. I knew she would understand my tears, because she, too, was crying. I live just twenty minutes from Heritage but never think of it being that close anymore. That was yesterday; today is today!

It's okay to be sad about those you have lost, it's okay to be sad about something you've lost. But when grief becomes a destructive force in your life, you must figure out a way to put it in perspective. Grief cannot bring anyone or anything back, no matter how much you cry, no matter how long you close yourself off from other people.

I have found the best way to deal with grief is to get busy doing other things for other people. Get involved in living! I watch so many TV shows about people who have lost children to horrible deaths. The ones who are able to go on with life are the ones who start working to prevent it from happening to other children, the ones that get busy and work toward laws being changed and new laws being passed. They get involved in doing for others, and in doing for others they are unconsciously helping their own grief.

In my times of desperation I read and reread Psalms 91. It never fails to comfort me. Isaiah 41:10 is also one of my favorite verses of the Bible. And once again I realize that this world is *not my home*. I'm only here for a while. Someday I will be going to my "real home" in Heaven, and there will be no losses there.

18.

Rejection and How to Handle It

Rejection can come in many forms—and I think I have experienced rejection in about every way possible. You'd think that after feeling rejected so many times you'd get used to it, but I don't think you ever really do. With every rejection there seems to come a feeling of self-doubt, a question of self-worth, and the feeling, "Well, I just must not be good enough."

It happened to me today. Recently, despite everything in me holding me back, I finally worked up the courage to ask a very wealthy friend of mine if he would help me financially to get back on Christian TV. He had told me that if I would get a budget together he would take a look at it. Perhaps I let my hopes get a little too high. I usually don't allow my hopes and expectations in life to grow too tall. I've learned over the years that they can be cut down very quickly, and the pain of that is too much for my heart to bear sometimes. So I always try to look at things realistically.

I faxed the TV budget to him after going over and over and over it to make sure it was cut to the bone. It certainly was not out of proportion. I let myself think that I had a fifty-fifty chance it would actually happen. My husband Roe wasn't quite so sure. I teased him about his lack of faith, and how with God all things are possible. Since he's a believer, I think my little mini-sermon worked on him, and he, too, began to feel that it wasn't out of the question.

When my friend hadn't called back for five days, Roe suggested that if he hadn't responded by the following day I needed to call him. I was dreading having to call such a busy man and bother him with something so small and insignificant to him. Of course, it wasn't small and insignificant to *me*. It meant starting over for me, a chance I have not had since PTL. The thought of his saying yes made me feel like my stomach was in my throat. The thought of his saying no . . . well, I tried not to think that thought.

So today the phone rang and Roe answered it. He came into the bedroom, where I was packing for a trip, and said it was my friend on the line. I felt like I was going to throw up. I wanted to hear what he had to say, and yet I didn't want to hear. But I knew I had to know sometime. So I took the phone, and a happy, positive voice said, "Hi, Tammy. How are you doing today?"

My friend and I exchanged small talk for a few minutes. My hopes were growing as we chatted—and then he said it:

"Tammy, I don't want to do this."

He proceeded to tell me that he had signed a contract a few days before, giving $4 million to another Christian organization. Four million dollars! All I needed to produce the show and buy airtime was less than $200,000. That would buy me six months. After six months, I felt in my heart, the show would be paying for itself.

He went on talking as if saying no to people were something he did every day. Perhaps it is. We exchanged family talk and said goodbye.

Now, to me, friendship is much more important than money. I never equate the two. In fact, I usually steer clear of rich people, because I don't ever want them to think I want to be their friend just because they have money. I feel much more comfortable around middle-class and working people.

So my first thought was, I shouldn't have asked my friend for this money. Why did I even think that he would say yes? My next thought was, It's over, my dream is over. A sadness came over me, a feeling of rejection by yet another friend, a feeling of inadequacy, and I could feel my self-confidence draining away like water down a sink.

Then the thought hit me: *Hey girl, put the plug in! Don't you dare let it all drain out.*

I certainly do not blame my friend. It's his money, and he has a right to support the things he wants to support. My questions will eventually fly away out of my mind and I'll be free again of my doubts. In the meantime, I keep chasing those doubts and questions away: Doesn't he think I'm good enough to do a talk show? I did one for thirty years! Is our friendship all one-sided, a figment of my imagination? What's $200,000 compared to $4 million? Maybe I'm not supposed to start over again. Does he not trust me?

Get away, bird—fly away! I will not allow you to make a nest in my hair!

The Bible says that when we're disappointed, hurt, angry, or feeling rejected, we need to think on things that are good. I always try to do that, and it really works. After all, nothing in life is worth giving up over.

The secret is to live one day at a time. Yesterday is gone; it's like a broken egg, it can never be put back together again. Today is all we have. None of us may even be here tomorrow.

> A person may fail many times, but he isn't a failure until he blames somebody or someone else.

I often think of Princess Di. I know she never in her wildest dreams thought she would die so young. She thought she had years of tomorrows left. I think of Elvis. And John Lennon—he never imagined he would walk out of his home and be shot to death. Marilyn Monroe, Judy Garland, John Kennedy Jr.—gone in an instant. The Bible says that life is but a vapor, it's like chasing the wind.

Yes, life is full of disappointments, dreams that never materialize, ambitions that are never realized, friends who let you down, relationships that fail, loved ones who die. Life has its share of loneliness it parcels out to those who will accept it, and a bountiful supply of unfairness.

But even so, I'm glad I made it this far. People always ask me what I would change about my life. They're dumbfounded when I say nothing. Because every bad thing that has happened to me has also brought about something good. Every bad thing has changed me for the better in some way. That which doesn't kill you makes you stronger.

Make a resolve today that no matter what happens, you are not going to let life get you down. You can make it! It's all about choice—*your* choice!

19.

The Song in My Heart

I think I've always had a song in my heart. I have always felt closest to God when I was singing. It was a way I could express myself to Him, express my deep love for Jesus. I remember as a little girl singing, "Oh, how I love Jesus, Oh, how I love Jesus, Oh, how I love Jesus, because He first loved me." My hand would be raised in the air, tears would be streaming down my face as I talked to God through song.

As a little girl in the Assembly of God church I would sing the song, "I'll go where you want me to go, dear Lord, o'er mountain or land or sea, I'll do what you want me to do, dear Lord, I'll be what you want me to be." No one ever meant those words more than I did. My entire little body cried out to be used by the Lord. I never dreamed where life would take me. I never dreamed that one day I'd sing to millions of people.

And I never dreamed that one day I would suffer so intensely that my song would be stilled. Yet even my own songs, ones I have sung for so many years, echoed over and over and over in my mind. I couldn't sing them, but I could hear them in my head. "Don't give up, you're on the brink of a miracle, don't give in, God is still on the throne, don't give up on the brink of a miracle, don't give in, remember you're not alone." Over and over and over it went in my head. I wanted to give up. I wanted to die. But that song in my head kept giving me hope.

For nearly two years I could not even read the Bible. I don't know why. Thank God I had memorized so much of it that it ran over and over in my head. Psalm 91, Romans 8:28—they swam around in my head and lodged in my hurting heart and gave me hope. I couldn't go to church; I no longer trusted the Christians. And if I did venture in the door of the church, I felt unwanted by the pastor, felt like a spectacle as people's eyes bored through me. My aching heart just could not take being in that environment.

Another thing that was hard for me to face in church, and it is still hard for me today: to sit in the congregation, when for thirty years Jim and I were the preachers. I feel a little lost yet today. I am always afraid people are pitying me—"Look what she lost." I don't want to be pitied! Of all the things I fear, I think I fear pity the most, as I *never* pity myself.

On TV, I used to sing the song "If Life Hands You a Lemon, Start Making Lemonade." It's all about how life has a way of knocking you down, but you have a choice: you can throw in the towel, or you can take the lemons life gives you and turn them into lemonade. It was a fun song to sing, but I never dreamed I'd have to *live* it.

But the song did give me courage. I made up my mind that I was not going to throw in the towel and run off and hide. The chorus of that song says we should thank God for even the

tough situations He gives us—to thank Him for the lemons—
and to praise Him for the day He made.

Those words are a challenge yet today. Thank God for the
situation. Uh huh! Praise Him for the day He made? That's a
little easier. But there were days when even that part was hard.

I remember feeling so far from God. I felt abandoned. I felt
as if the prayers I so desperately prayed hit the ceiling of the
room I was praying in and fell back down, nearly crushing me
with doubt. God, where are you? I felt so numb. I would pace
back and forth in the rooms of my house like a nervous cat. I
could never just sit down—if I did, I would think, and above
all else I had to keep bad thoughts away. I would eventually
end up aimlessly playing my piano. Half the time I would not
even know what I was playing until my mind would begin to
sing along.

Blessed assurance, Jesus is mine!
Oh what a foretaste of glory divine!
Heir of salvation, purchased of God,
Born of His Spirit, washed in His blood.
This is my story, this is my song,
Praising my Savior all the day long;
This is my story, this is my song,
Praising my Savior all the day long.

Tears streaming down my face, falling onto the piano keys,
making them so slippery I could hardly keep my fingers on
them, I realized that I was "praising the Lord!" I would go from
one song to another. "Let me touch Him, let me touch Jesus,
let me touch Him as He passes by. Let me touch Him, let me

touch Jesus, so that others may live and not die. Oh, to be His hand extended, reaching out to the oppressed. Let me touch Him, let me touch Jesus, so that others may know and be blessed."

I wanted to be the hands of Jesus extended. I wanted, as we had done so many years on television, to touch people. Yet it seemed to me that I no longer had a vehicle to reach the world for Jesus. I was just a hurting person, like the ones I wanted to reach out to, sitting at home, not able to go to church or even read my Bible. Would my life ever count for Jesus again? Could I or would I ever sing again? I looked at my record albums, twenty-five of them, staring up at me. I remembered recording each one—remembered being so grateful to God for allowing me to put my music on albums. I remembered the anointing of the Lord I felt in the recording studio as I sang the songs, sometimes having to stop because I couldn't sing and cry at the same time. I wondered, Will I ever make another album?

I have a longing to do another one someday, but that's in God's hands. And they're not called albums anymore, they're now CDs. I have since had almost all my albums transferred to CDs. I didn't want to lose the songs that literally kept me alive during the worst part of my life. I listen to them sometimes, a bittersweet experience. I can still feel the presence of the Lord in those songs, I still am caught up in praise and worship when I hear one of those old songs being played. And I still feel the longing to sing them again sweep over my very soul.

But Christian television doesn't want me, and secular television does not want my songs. But they still go over and over in my head, encouraging me, the way people tell me my songs encouraged them when I sang them on PTL. The Bible says "Jesus Christ, the same yesterday, today and forever."

My daughter told me a story I shall never forget. She walked into her house one day and her girlfriend was there. She had one of my CDs playing so loud that you could hear it clear outside. Tammy Sue said, "Mom, I was so discouraged that day, and the last thing I wanted to do was to listen to you sing. I went over to turn the music off, when all of a sudden I felt the presence of the Lord, Mom. I began to cry and worship the Lord as my friend Diana was already doing." She said all of a sudden the discouragement and the terrible depression that she had been living in for weeks lifted. She called me sobbing! "Mom, I'm free, I'm free!" We were both crying by that time. And I realized that my music will live on—even if I never record another word—in the hearts of those who need it.

About a week ago, I once again witnessed God using my music. My neighbor and good friend had something so sad happen in her family. She just could not face the problem and went and got my album *Old Hymns of the Church,* which I had given her months before. She said that she and her husband have been playing that album day and night, going on days now. She said, "Tammy, your songs bring such peace and hope and comfort to me." She said she transferred the album to her computer so that it never shuts off. I went to her house the other day and I heard my voice coming from that computer, singing the songs of the redeemed. And I thanked the Lord. I was still able to minister, and I wasn't even on Christian TV.

Thank you, God!

20.

The Power of Agreement

The power of agreement is awesome. The Bible says that one can put one thousand to flight, but two can put ten thousand to flight. So simply by agreeing with one other person, you can be ten times more effective.

I have found in life that I am much braver if someone is with me, encouraging me in whatever I am doing. Things that I would never think of doing alone because of fear or doubt become doable or bearable when I have someone with me. Someone to cheer you on works like magic! Your confidence level increases so much. Your tolerance to pain even increases if someone is there to tell you it's going to be all right, or that there will soon be an end to the pain, or just to soothe your nerves by talking you down or up, whatever the need at the time may be.

I think of women giving birth. I have watched so many births on TV, and everyone is standing around giving encouragement to the woman. You can do it, push, push, push! I think of sports events, particularly track. A runner will be just at the point of giving up and giving out when he hears everyone screaming, "Come on, you can make it! Just a little farther! Come on, come on!" And right before your eyes that runner will form a new determination, get an extra spurt of strength and energy. At the point of possible defeat, he or she will spring back and win. Adrenaline begins to flow when we know people are on our side, rooting us on, letting us know they have faith in us.

> It takes two to fight. If one refuses, there is no fight!

I do one-woman shows around the country. Even in the best of circumstances, my self-confidence can lag. On a recent night, I was appearing in Los Angeles and had been waiting an hour to go on when I was suddenly given the cue that it was showtime. My heart began to pound as the lights were dimmed, and a huge spotlight finally found me standing in the back of the auditorium. As my music came up, I started down the aisle of the packed theater and began to sing—into a dead microphone!

In a split second, all sorts of negative thoughts whirled through my mind. This is LA! What are the critics going to say? I have close friends in the audience who are seeing me for the first time in years—what will they think?

It's amazing how much can go through your mind in such a short time.

But then, suddenly, God came through for me. No, the microphone did not start working—the *people who loved me* did. They started cheering, "Tammy! Tammy! Tammy! We love you!"

In that second, we all came into agreement. They were with me, and I was going to make it even if everything went wrong.

And it did.

I finally made it to the stage, laughing all the way. What else could I do? The mike went in and out the entire evening, there wasn't enough light onstage for me to see my cue cards, my contact lenses were not working because of an infection in my eye, I forgot the end of a joke I was telling and could not remember it until the very end of the show. . . . It was just one awful thing after another.

But I think it ended up being one of the best shows I've ever done. Why? Because the audience knew what was happening and was in agreement with me that no matter what happened they were with me until the bitter end. And they constantly cheered me on each time another calamity befell me.

> Right is right even if everyone is against it, and wrong is wrong even if everyone is for it.

That night after the show, I stood onstage for nearly two hours autographing photos of myself. Everyone wanted me to write things like "You can make it!" and "If life hands you a lemon, make lemonade!"

It's so funny. All the day before I had felt led to pray, pray, pray for the show that night. I always pray before everything I do, but that day was different. It nagged at me. See, God knew what was going to go wrong that night, and He didn't choose to make it go right; He chose to let me learn a valuable lesson. Things could have gone completely differently. In Los Angeles, audiences are used to seeing the best shows in the country. But everyone knows what it feels like when things go wrong, and they graciously put themselves in my place and helped me through the rough spots. They were as much a part of that show as I was. I feel that is exactly what God intended for that night: hundreds of people agreeing that they were going to stay with me until the end. Yay, God!

And what did the critics say? That the way I handled it reminded them of Lucille Ball. Lucy! What higher compliment could I have ever received?

Romans 8:28 says, "For we know that all things work together for good to them that love the Lord and to them that are the called according to His purpose." That verse will *never* fail you.

Now, the power of agreement also works when it comes to doing evil. Even the devil knows about this power. Even the devil knows that two people together will do things that one alone would never even think of doing.

I often say if one refuses to fight there is no fight. If one party refuses to argue, that stops it right there. If two are together, and one refuses to listen to gossip, that ends it. But if they are in agreement to engage in gossip, they can start a fire that can lead to disaster. Many people's lives have been forever destroyed because two people started talking and agreeing.

Riots start when the second person decides to join the one who is attempting to cause trouble. If you don't want to be that second person, all you have to do is just say no. Just walk away. Refuse to join in agreement. Refuse to give that person the power he or she needs to make evil happen.

It took the power of agreement to destroy the world's largest Christian TV network. Lies were told and believed. If those lies had fallen on deaf ears, they never could have spread. Instead, one man told lies, convinced others to agree with him, and in turn they were able to convince an entire nation that what they were saying was truth. So I have seen the power of *sinful* agreement. I will never, as long as I live, forget those men in suits walking into the room where Jim and I were sitting, all in agreement that they were going to take over the PTL Television Network. Before they left they would have everything they needed to do just that. Through one man's lies and deceit they spun a web of destruction. One person alone could never have accomplished that. But when those men came together in agreement, their power grew tenfold. Christians, think of that the next time you're tempted to agree with another person, positively or negatively. Remember it works both ways.

Jim Bakker lost PTL because he inadvertently agreed with those men. They declared that because of Jim's one-night stand with a woman, he needed to give up his place on the board of directors of PTL for six weeks. And Jim agreed. He agreed that he had sinned, and he agreed to let these men "help" him handle the public's reaction to his sin. That's how Jim was drawn into the power of agreement with those men. And the power went directly into their hands. It was one of the clearest examples of the power of agreement I have ever witnessed.

If only Jim had agreed with me instead of them, he would never have lost PTL. Not that I am anything special, but I knew in my heart that what they were doing was wrong and begged Jim not to give up his place on the board of directors. Our power of agreement would have prevented that tragedy.

21.

Facades

Webster's dictionary defines the word facade as "1. The front or main face of a building 2. An imposing appearance concealing something inferior."

The Disney people are the masters of facade. They're capable of taking an ordinary building and turning it into "magic." They turn stark buildings into castles, haunted houses, theme restaurants; facades cover rides like Pirates of the Caribbean, It's a Small World; facades cover everything. Facades turn simple stores into Hawaiian villages, Mexican villages, Italian villas. They even cover their construction sites with facades, turning messes into lands of wonder. There is no limit to what they can do when building a facade. A facade can take something ugly on the outside and turn it into a thing of beauty.

But none of the fantasy is real. Disney is just that—fantasy. If you took down the facades at Disneyland and Disney World, you'd find ordinary buildings. Disneyland and Disney World are just wonderful figments of our imagination. It works because we want it to work. We don't want to think what's behind all the facades.

And that's fine—*when it's Disney.*

I began to think about people I know who cover themselves with a facade. They cover up their "true selves." They're something different from what others see. We can only see the outside, we believe what they're saying, we're incapable of seeing past most people's facade. We *want* to believe in people's facades. We do not want to think that people are capable of deceiving us; we want to believe that everyone is good and honest and true. We don't want to look beyond the facade for fear of what we might find.

I have had too much personal experience with people living behind facades. It has caused me to look beyond the obvious.

Two young men had been hired by our ministry. They had come highly recommended. They were very personable, they were hard workers, and we immediately accepted these two young men as part of our family. We loved them like family. We trusted them like family. They were part of our ministry for many years before we discovered they were hiding behind a facade. Both young men ended up in prison. Unbeknownst to Jim, they had been taking money from the ministry for years, but because of the wonderful facade they wore, we had not one clue. I still can't believe it today, so many years later. I try to look back and figure it out. Now that I know, hindsight reveals what should have been obvious. But somehow, when you're a Christian and working around Christians, you don't want to look further than what you see and what you hear. You so badly want to believe people are what they say they are.

The Bible calls someone who wears a facade a "wolf in sheep's clothing." I believe Christians are more susceptible to being deceived by a facade than the rest of the world. We believe that no matter how bad a person was before they accepted Christ as their Savior, they can be redeemed and therefore rehabilitated. So if they say they've been changed and made a new person in Christ Jesus, who are we to question them?

The Bible makes it plain to us that we are able, through the Holy Spirit, to discern the spirit. That our spirit will bear witness with the spirit of a true believer. But what happens, I believe, is that we get too busy going about our daily lives to take time to pray, to take time to read the Word, to take time to talk to the Lord. And our minds are so caught up with other things that we don't listen to "that still, small voice" within us that can warn us of impending danger.

Then there are the times when God Himself warns us of impending danger; He causes a question to arise within us. But we chase the feeling away because it's just easier not to heed the warning, or we say to ourselves that it cannot be true. We don't *want* it to be true, so we ignore that small voice within us.

That happened to me too. And again it was about someone the ministry had hired. He was a leader in our denomination. He was well thought of by everyone we talked to. He had charisma, great charisma. And Jim needed help running a ministry that was fast becoming bigger than he ever dreamed it could be.

I agreed that this man was the perfect man for the job. He was hired, and for a time we all thought he was God's gift to our ministry. Then a still, small voice began to speak to my heart. I could not get away from it. I went to Jim and told him what I felt God was telling me. But the man was taking a heavy load off Jim's tired shoulders, and he was unwilling to hear what I was saying.

Then God began speaking to others in our ministry about this man. They went to Jim, and he was unwilling to listen to their pleas to check into things this man was doing. He told them to prove the accusations before they came to him with them again.

If a facade is well built, it's hard to look behind! And this man's facade was very well built. By the time Jim realized God really was talking to people's hearts, it was too late. This man also went to jail. We loved this man and his family, we trusted this fellow minister of the Gospel, we trusted him with our lives and with our ministry. He, too, was part of our family. Why didn't we see through the facade before we hired him to run the ministry? We were not listening, not listening to that still, small voice of the Holy Spirit.

It was fatal for our ministry, for this man joined together with another man who wore a facade. Again, the scriptures come to my mind: "One can put a thousand to flight; two can put ten thousand to flight." So when he joined with this other man, the odds increased by tenfold that Heritage USA—our ministry we had spent thirty years building—could be taken away. That scripture works for Christians and the non-believer alike. Like gravity, it works for everyone!

The man's facade was that of a compassionate savior, filled with love for Jim and his ministry. He came to Jim with a story that so embarrassed and frightened Jim that he could not hear that warning voice. Fear had taken away Jim's ability to listen to what God was trying to say to him.

Nine years before, Jim made a mistake. He has since apologized to us. But this man with the well-built facade saw an opportunity to take over the world's largest television ministry. He called Jim personally and told him he had heard about this mistake and said that someone was going to release it to the media. However, he also said that if Jim would turn the ministry over to him for a few weeks, he felt he could stop any stories from coming out.

He flew in his private jet to Palm Springs, where I had just been released from the hospital with near-fatal pneumonia, and told Jim and me to meet him in the local hotel so he could help us. He took us in a private room, put his arms around us and cried like a baby, saying he had helped other ministries through similar situations and he wanted to help us. He said, "I don't want your ministry. I'd never hurt you and Tammy. I only want to help you over this rough spot." He convinced Jim to sign the ministry over to his care—temporarily, he said. He said Jim would have it back in six weeks.

> People are like tea bags: If you want to find out what's inside of them, just drop them in hot water.

(That never happened, and to this day this man denies that he ever said it.) I begged Jim not to do that. The voice inside me was not a still, small voice: It was a large, booming voice warning me. I knew what they were doing but could not convince Jim, because he thought these men wouldn't betray him. Fear and embarrassment were ruling his mind, and he could not hear that still, small voice warning him. He could not even hear my loud, booming voice begging him not to give up his place on the board of directors!

This man went to the media and told horrible lies for days and days on end. He said there were millions of dollars missing—that was a lie! He said that Jim had mishandled finances—that was a lie! He said Jim had stolen millions from the ministry—that was a lie! He said that Jim was a homosexual—

that was a lie! This man went into beautiful Heritage USA and took the mailing list and used it for his own ministry. He raised millions of dollars saying it was for paying PTL's bills, but mysteriously the millions of dollars never went to PTL. He took truckloads of furniture out of the beautiful Heritage Grand Hotel. He had thousands and thousands of dollars' worth of books that Jim had written, and thousands of dollars' worth of records I had made, and had huge holes dug and buried them. He forced our three thousand workers to sign a paper saying that they could not contact Jim or Tammy in any way or they would be fired. My own mother worked at PTL in the mailroom and begged him to let her keep her job. He fired her on the spot. Within six months of his taking over PTL, he threw it into bankruptcy. I will never figure out how he managed to do that.

This man managed to hold onto Heritage USA and PTL for about nine months, when he abruptly left. He had filed a plan through bankruptcy court to reorganize, but the court approved a competing plan Roe Messner and the creditors filed. This man knew he could not win and left that day. He had finally been foiled. His facade had been removed. Finally! And the world saw who he really was. At least those who were willing to see.

Because of the lies of two men who had joined together in agreement, Jim Bakker was sent to prison. He was given a forty-five-year sentence. At fifty years old, that was life for him. What did he do, you say? *He did not go to prison for stealing from the ministry or embezzling from the ministry.* Jim is the most honest man I've ever known. They said that he went to prison for overbooking a hotel, something hotels do every day, as do the airlines. They said he used the mail, the airways, and phone system to do this, therefore it was a federal offense.

I do not have to stand up for Jim Bakker. I have been re-married for ten years now. But I was married to Jim for thirty years and I knew Jim's character. He would never steal from anyone, much less his own ministry. Jim served five years of the forty-five-year sentence.

People say where are the millions that were said to be missing? Go visit Heritage USA in North Carolina. There are millions of dollars' worth of beautiful building still sitting there. They are not being taken care of by the men who purchased the property; they are rotting away—beautiful hotels empty, a huge TV studio, the roof now caving in; buildings being sold off for almost nothing; a building burning down mysteriously. I wonder who should really have gone to prison.

I have forgiven the men with the facades. I had to, or I would die a bitter old woman. And the Bible says if we do not forgive those who have sinned against us, God will not forgive us of our sins. I would rather be right before the Lord than anything in this world. I gave those men to God many years ago, and I leave them with Him. God is a just God!

God Loves You Just the Way You Are—He Really Does

22.

Looking Good and Self-Esteem

All of my life I have been self-deprecating. I have always felt that if I put myself down first I wouldn't have to suffer the humiliation of somebody else doing it. When someone cracked a joke about me I would be the first to laugh, and I'd laugh the loudest. I refused to let anyone know how much it hurt me.

Self-esteem has been my number-one battle in my life. I have always thought that everyone else could do anything better than me—that every woman was in some way prettier than me. If it wasn't their face, it was a body part that looked better than mine. I am very short and have always hated my little, fat legs and my fat ankles. I always admired women with long shapely legs and skinny ankles.

My idea of a perfect woman is Olivia Newton John in the

movie *Grease*. When that movie came out I vowed that I was going to lose weight and have a figure exactly like Olivia Newton John's. At the time I had just had my second child and was feeling particularly unsure of my looks. So I joined an exercise class, lost thirty pounds and twenty-nine inches. I looked fantastic! I got me a pair of black spandex pants, stood in front of a full-length mirror, and for the first time in my life felt like I looked as good as any other woman. Very tiny but very shapely. I wrote a book with Jim on how to lose weight and keep it off. And I did. I kept it off for over five years. I learned at that time the things that put weight on me, and I have never forgotten. I learned that exercise is essential, and for five years I felt guilty if I didn't exercise every day.

Losing weight made me fall in love with clothes, and I still love them today. Not expensive clothes, just clothes in general. I was just as happy in something from Kmart as I was in something from Saks Fifth Avenue. When you're on TV every day, people expect you to look different on each show, and I did my best to please the people. People would tell me they tuned into our TV program "to see what Tammy was wearing." Putting clothes together was something I was and still am very good at. I don't care what the critics say. I know when a woman looks well dressed, and I did.

I have worn high heels since I was thirteen years old. I can remember walking down dirt roads, going to church, wearing three-inch heels. They made my four-foot eleven-inch frame look taller, I thought. I still wear high heels every day of my life. My legs hurt if I walk in flat shoes for very long. I still feel high heels make everything look better.

I also fell in love with shoulder pads. I always thought the ladies in the 1940s were so beautiful with their big shoulders and tiny waistlines. But that went out of style, and it was years before shoulder pads finally came back in. And when they did, I was first in line. (I will never forget the first time I found out you could actually buy them over the counter at department stores.) I have never liked the ones they put in clothes at the factory. I take them out and wear my own.

I still have boxes of shoulder pads that I purchased years ago, just in case they went out of style again and I might not be able to get them. I will wear them until the day I die! Again, I feel they make me look taller and thinner. In my eyes they just finish a look, like a hat finishes a look. An ordinary little t-shirt becomes a special item if you add shoulder pads. Clothes have done so much to help my self-esteem, be it right or wrong.

I don't know if you're born with self-esteem or you develop it as you go. I think it must be a developed trait. Or maybe you *are* born with it and people knock it out of you. I don't know. Then you have to learn who you are, you have to learn to like yourself in spite of what people say. So maybe it's also a learned trait.

I think makeup did as much to hurt my self-esteem as it did to build it. Does that seem like a contradiction? Maybe. On one hand, I felt that I looked so much better wearing makeup, and there-

People often ask me why so much makeup I wear. I tell them my face is a canvas, ready to paint, always there.
They ask me why I wear my wigs brown, blond, and red. I tell them I get easily bored and want to change my head!

fore my self-esteem grew in leaps and bounds when I began wearing it. On the other hand, people began to make fun of me when I started to wear makeup. They would cruelly put me down, calling me a clown, saying that I applied it with a paint-brush. Of course they blew everything out of proportion by drawing cartoons of me with eyelashes blowing in the wind, or of me holding a trowel or paint cans filled with makeup. I have been made fun of by the best that Hollywood has to offer, plus the general public of know-it-alls. But I have held up despite their cruel taunts. I feel I look better with it than without it, and after all it's my right to make that call.

Similary, singing, like makeup, has both helped and hurt my self-esteem. I have always loved to sing. It's a tremendous way to communicate. Here again, I am always self-deprecating. I may not be a good singer, but I'm *loud* and I stay on key. Exactly on key! And I sing with passion. Singing makes me feel close to God. Singing allows me to say things to people that I can't put into words any other way. People either hate my voice and think I sing awfully or they love my voice. There seems to be no in-between. I continue to sing in spite of what anyone says. Singing is part of who I am. It always has been. I have recorded twenty-five albums in my life and have two gold records hanging on the wall in my living room. If people don't like my singing, they don't have to buy my CDs.

Something interesting recently happened when *The Jimmy Kimmel Show* on ABC sent me as their correspondent to a MENSA convention in Orlando. As usual, my low self-esteem kicked into gear, but I kicked it right back. I jumped into interview mode with both feet. For the first time, I actually didn't care what people thought. Yeah for me! I have been doing live television for thirty-five years, and I felt I could do it about as well as anyone else could. I was not surprised that they asked me to be their correspondent; I was surprised that they seemingly did not consider my age. Now *that* is a self-esteem builder. Hollywood generally looks for the sexy, under-thirty "beautiful people."

But more than that, the MENSA experience allowed me to let myself go and really enjoy myself. I don't know why, but I decided to throw caution to the wind. I joined in the MENSA belly-dancing class! I have never danced in my life. It took more courage than I knew I had to let loose and allow myself to make a fool of myself—and to allow other people to call me a fool and not care. I was set free that day of so many hang-ups. I allowed myself to let go in spite of what people would say, and just have good clean fun. Belly-dancing! I think it's the most fun I have ever had. What a delight, after all these years, to dance. I think of David, and how he danced before the Lord. I think of how, when I was going through the worst nightmares of my life, I opened my Bible in desperation, and the scripture verse said "you shall once again laugh with joy" (Luke 6:21–22).

Self-Esteem

As I've gotten older I have learned some mental tricks that have helped me immensely in the self-esteem department. Maybe you need to learn them too:

* God made me unique. I am a one of a kind!

* God gave me the face He wanted me to have, and it's just fine!

* God gave me the voice He wanted me to have, and it's just fine too.

* I am *not* an inferior person. I am just fine.

* There are people with fewer "attributes" than I have who have been very successful in life.

* I am just as good as anyone else!

* It doesn't matter what the critics say. It's just talk, and talk is cheap.

* My opinion is just as valuable as anyone else's.

* I have wonderful common sense.

* I have the right to my own style.

* It is none of my business what other people think of me. It doesn't matter.

* I love God and people with all my heart, and that is all that really matters.

23.

Always Someone Better

I love to be around people with self-confidence. They have an air about them that rubs off a little, and it makes you feel self-confident too. When you're with a self-confident person you feel that together you can conquer anything.

Self-confident people seem to lack fear; they don't seem to care what people think; they dare to be just who they are. They may not be handsome or beautiful, they may not be rich or stylish, they may not be what we call at "the top of the ladder" of life, but they seem satisfied just being themselves. And so you don't notice all the things that may be missing. Their self-confidence overwhelms all the missing things, and all you see is a person you like to be around, a person who has it all together, a person you wish you could be like.

Whether their self-confidence is real or just an act, it still works. This is interesting to me. I once knew a famous woman preacher. She had traveled the world preaching and singing and was, I thought, the greatest woman, the most self-confident woman, the most charismatic woman I had ever met. I could not wait for her to walk out on the stage. Could not wait for her to sit down at the piano in that huge auditorium and start to sing, could not wait until she stood to begin ministering. My husband and I got very close to this woman, and I learned a lesson I shall never forget. Before each service, she would be in the restroom vomiting. She would be that nervous. But the minute she hit that stage, you would not believe it was the same woman. She exuded self-confidence, not fear; she was powerful, full of authority. She drew you in.

I learned so much from Sister Fern Olson. I loved her so. But I learned that even she had self-doubts from time to time. That she was only human, just like me. What is more, in private she admitted that to have courage and self-confidence is a choice—something you choose to have and be every day.

Everyone thinks I am so self-confident. I laugh when I hear people say that they were a little afraid of me before they got to know me. I don't think there's anyone who has fought a lack of self-confidence more than I have.

I have never felt tall enough, thin enough, intelligent enough, or pretty enough. Then when you get older you never feel young enough. And if you think life in general will make you feel that way, try having to be on television every day, where you're judged from the minute you walk on the set until the minute you leave the set. Christian television is bad enough, but secular television is *brutal*. Women in particular live in fear of keeping their jobs on television. There is always someone younger, prettier, and more talented who has more of an edge than you do.

So you ask, How do you build your self-confidence, and how in the world do you keep it?

For one thing, believe in yourself and don't let anyone or anything take that away from you. God made you who you are, and you are as well made as anyone else. You were fashioned by a top designer! The same God who made Marilyn Monroe, Clark Gable, Elvis, Princess Di, Mother Teresa, Billy Graham . . . you fill in some of the people you most admire or think you could never live up to. The same God made us all. We are all made out of "the same old dirt."

Yes, some people may be more beautiful or handsome than you. They may be more talented or more intelligent than you. But there's only one you! And nobody, no matter how hard they try, can be you, or do the job in this world you're supposed to do. Never try to be somebody else. A carbon copy is never as good or worth as much as the original. Be an original! Dare to be an original! Dare to be you!

People have always tried to change me. Always. I talk too loud, I'm too silly, I am too emotional, I trust too much, I dress too wildly, I wear too much makeup, my eyelashes are too long, my hair never stays the same color for long. You would be surprised by the things people say. If I took to heart the things people say, I'd never walk out of the house again, much less go back on television.

Everyone has an opinion. Anyone can talk. Talk is cheap. It takes no intelligence to talk. But it does take intelligence to *keep your mouth shut.*

It's funny to me. Some people say I can't sing a lick. Others say I'm their favorite singer and they love to hear me sing. Some people think I'm ugly; then there are people who think I'm *so cute*. Of course I listen to *them*.

There are people who say I don't have a lick of sense; then there are those who say I'm very intelligent. People say I'm too heavy for my small frame. Others say I'm just right, and still others say I should gain a little weight. My girlfriend said that to me just the other day. I just lost about twenty-five pounds and she thought it was a little too much.

So how do I process all these opinions in my head? I don't bother! What people think of me is none of my business. The only important opinions in this world are what *I* think of me and what God thinks of me.

When Jim and I lost PTL and the whole world seemed to be against us; when we were on every television newscast, in every newspaper and magazine, and there was not one positive word being uttered about us, how did I make it through that?

First of all, I protected myself by not watching or listening to any of it. I did not watch it on TV, I did not read anything in print. I would go to the grocery store and pass by the magazine rack. At times I was tempted to pick up a magazine with our picture plastered across the front—but I knew if I did I would not be able to live. My heart was already so broken I had to protect it from further hurt. I had to protect my mind. I could not allow negative words, spoken or printed, to invade my thinking and ultimately destroy me forever.

We all know our limitations, and we should not be embarrassed by them. We just need to know and work within our limitations. There are certain limitations we can overcome by the sheer will to do so. There are others we are created with and must accept. And each of us basically knows what our own human limitations are.

What are some of my limitations? Emotionally, I am hurt very easily. I trust people too much and too quickly—not as much anymore as I used to, but I still trust too much. I'm a bit gullible. I'm probably a bit naive. I have a tendency to be too quick to express my opinion. And I have a hard time changing that opinion. When I'm hurting, I want to hide from people. I never want to bother other people, so I wait until they make the move to be with me rather than make a move myself. I don't take criticism well; it hurts too much. I have never had much self-esteem.

So how have I dealt with my limitations? When I get hurt I tell myself, "Tammy, get over it." It may take a few days, but dealing with the hurt and staying light about it, instead of allowing the heaviness of it to crush me, helps me overcome the pain. I don't allow myself to dwell on what's hurt me in the past. It's done, over with, and there's nothing I can do about the hurts of yesterday. I choose to move ahead and let them go.

And it *is* a choice. With God all things are possible. He wants to "renew our minds" if we will let Him. "Old things pass away, and behold all things become new" when we give it all to Jesus.

So when the hurt hits you, as it sometimes will, just say, "Jesus, I give that hurt to you, and I give the person who hurt me to you." Then chase the thought from your mind.

How? Get busy doing something, helping someone, whatever works for you. I have seen hurt people destroyed because they would not let go of the hurt. My daughter once told me, "Mother, quit obsessing." I never forgot that. We can learn from our kids.

So quit obsessing over the hurts in your life and move on.

What about trusting people too much? You must remember that we are living in a world of sin. I have always thought that

everybody was basically good. That if I would not do something, they wouldn't either. That their convictions were the
same as mine.

I was wrong. The Bible says that we are born into sin, and
unless we have asked God to forgive us of that sinful nature,
the devil will have control of our minds and heart. But I have
found out that Christians can be very cruel. They can be very
judgmental, even though the Bible says to judge not lest we be
judged. So trusting people is still an issue with me. I'm very
careful whom I trust and have a tendency now to make people
prove themselves to me before I can form friendships. I don't
believe half of what anyone tells me, and I've come to think
that's a wise policy.

Be careful. The people I most trusted have most betrayed my
trust in them. And believe it or not, it was usually over money.
My friends, or people I thought were friends, betrayed our
whole family for money. But remember this: Money is soon
gone, and you have lost something so much more important
than money when you lose a good friend. I can still love a friend
who has betrayed me, but it's very hard ever to trust them again,
and I remain guarded around them. Unlike God, we can forgive, but we do not have the ability to forget. That is divine.
(This is why we must always be careful what we speak. Words
can never be taken back—never. And words spoken in anger,
jealousy, or whatever can be forgiven but not forgotten. I always
remember that. Some of the kindest words are the ones left unspoken.)

I learned a great lesson about money. When Jim and I were
young and traveling the evangelical circuit, we were hardly ever
paid more than enough to cover just our meals and gas for our
car. There was one time, near Christmas, when we needed a lit-

tle extra money. I told Jim, "Don't worry, I'll call Aunt Gin." She was like a mom to me. So I called, and when I asked her if we could borrow some money she said, "No, Tammy, I will *give* you the money you need, but I will not *loan* you the money. There is nothing that will destroy a friendship as fast as money." I would live to see the truth of that.

Think about it. You loan a friend money in good faith, confident that your "good friend" will pay you back at the agreed time. You continue to be good friends, and then that loan comes due. You hint around, trying not to make them mad at you, reminding them that they need to pay you back. Well, they don't have it right now, but they will soon. How many times have you heard that? In good faith you continue to believe them. But the longer it takes, the more edgy your friendship with them becomes. You trusted them enough to loan them the money, but now you're hurt and starting to get angry and disappointed in them. On their side, they're now wanting to avoid you, because they know they're doing wrong by not getting the money back to you when they said they would.

Generally, if the money is never paid back the friendship will suffer irreparable damage. I know many people who were once best friends who will no longer even speak to each other over money. I know two brothers who have not spoken in years, because one owes the other thousands of dollars and has owed it for years. The one won't speak because he's hurt, the other will not speak because he is embarrassed by the fact he has never paid his debt.

These situations are so sad, destroyed friendships are so sad, especially when it's over something as trite as money. As a result, I will *never* loan anyone money. If I *give* it instead, then I stay happy. If I give it to them I will never have to worry about being disappointed in that person if I never get it back. You see, I know my limitations. I know the anger I feel when people don't keep their word. I know my inability to forget. So I work with my limitations. By doing that I protect myself from myself.

Then there's that bad habit I have of expressing my opinion a little quicker and louder than I mean to. It seems to just jump out. I'm learning to keep my mouth shut, but it's been a hard row to hoe, as my grandmother used to say.

> Don't get too impressed with yourself. We're all made out of the same old dirt.

My husband Roe has helped me with this problem, and he doesn't even know it. I watch him and listen to him when he's doing business. I don't know how he keeps his cool and keeps his mouth shut when he knows that what the other party is saying is dead wrong, but he does. That fascinates me. He never raises his voice, he just lets them talk, and then in his calm, soft-spoken way tells them what he thinks. He never insists he's right; he just calmly tells them his opinion. It works every time. Like magic. Or is it because, as the Bible says, "a soft answer turneth away wrath"? Hmmm . . . could be the Bible really works!

I am learning, and I am practicing. I'm not really good at it yet, but if you're working on it I think you get points.

Now, about wanting to run and hide when I'm hurting and not reaching out to friends who truly want to help . . . Well, I really don't have an answer to that yet. But I'm still young (at heart). Sometimes I think we're afraid to ask people for help for fear that they'll refuse, or that they'll make up excuses so they don't have to help. And this is not always so. I have friends I know would come at any moment and stay with me until I could be by myself again. When my mom died I was out of my mind with grief. It was a sudden death and a terrible shock to me. I was so deeply in shock I could not remember that my daughter lived in the same town as my mom.

It was early in the morning when I received the call. I had taken a friend to the airport and come back home to get another hour of sleep. The telephone woke me up. When I answered it, a voice said, "Is this Tammy Bakker? This is the undertaker calling. Your mother is lying here dead in a chair. What do you want us to do with her?"

My mind actually seemed to go dead when I heard that. Yet I could hear myself screaming, I don't know, I don't know, what do you usually do when someone dies? Realizing he had made a mistake in the way he had talked to me, the undertaker softened his voice and said, "Tammy, don't you worry. We'll take her to the hospital and that will give you time to make a decision."

Make a decision? I was thousands of miles away and had no money to even buy an airline ticket. Whom could I call, what should I do? I was frantic. Frantic with grief, frantic that I could not remember the names of anyone in Charlotte, NC. (I was in Palm Springs, CA.) I walked around the house screaming, "God help me, please help me remember the name of someone!" After about a half hour of pacing and crying and praying for help, my aunt Gin's name came to me. I ran to the phone and dialed her number. She could not understand what I was saying I was crying so hard. Then came the voice of reason. She had always been the voice of reason in my life. She said in a firm but loving voice, "Tammy, speak so that I can understand you. Slow down and calm down. Now, what's happened?"

Hearing her familiar voice somehow brought me out of the

frenzy I was in. She told me to first of all check and make sure someone was not playing a joke on me—she knew the cruelty of people. That made sense to me, and at the same time offered a small ray of hope that maybe, just maybe, Mom wasn't really dead. Aunt Gin told me to call Tammy Sue, my daughter, and to ask her to go see if it really was my mom. I went into little-girl mode, doing exactly what Aunt Gin told me to do, almost like a robot. The little ray of hope that it might be a joke gave me time to calm down and get my mind back.

I called Tammy Sue, and she said very calmly that she would take care of going to the hospital and checking Mom's house, whatever needed to be done. In a few minutes she called me back and said that Mom was in the hospital. She had died. Tammy Sue was on her way to go see for herself.

About an hour passed and the phone rang again. It was Sue. "Mom, I saw Grandma. Mom, she looked so cute! They had put pink lipstick on her, Mom." We both started laughing a bit hysterically. My mom had never worn lipstick in her life. We both knew how funny that would be to her. She was such a funny lady anyway. She would have loved it.

The laughter turned into tears again, but this time they were not hysterical tears, just tears of great sadness. And I was crying with my precious daughter, who knew me and understood me as no one else ever could.

I called my aunt Gin back. She walked me through what I should do next, step by step. We had Mom flown to International Falls, where she had lived all her life. Grandma and Grandpa Fairchild were buried there, as were two of her brothers. We wanted her near them. She took her first airplane flight that day—but she wasn't afraid! She was already with Jesus, safe in His great big arms.

This was one time I reached out to a friend. I called my friend Emma, but she wasn't home, so I left a tearful message on her answering machine. "Emma, my mom has died and I hurt so bad. I just wanted to let you know." It wasn't an hour later when Emma Howard walked in my front door, carrying her bags, to stay as long as I needed her. For three days she talked about her mom, who had also died. She slept in my bed with me so I didn't have to be alone. I was not married at the time, so I was completely alone. If she had not been there for me I hate to think what it would have been like. God had Emma be there for me.

Other friends paid my way home to International Falls. In fact, they came and got me and flew with me, and then flew back with me. My friends did not forget me. They were there for me in my time of greatest need. All I had to do was tell them that Mom died and they took care of everything else for me.

That's the way God is too. All we have to do is call on the name of Jesus and He will be there for us. But we have to have enough courage to call His name. He will be there for us immediately, and He'll send whatever help we need to make it through times of crisis in our lives. He will have everyone in the right place at the right time to be His arms extended. Emma was God's arm extended that awful day.

God will help you face all your limitations. He will help you to work with what He gave you or didn't give you. But remember: *God didn't make no junk.* He has never made junk! You are special to Him, even if you aren't special to anyone else. He loves you more than anyone could ever love you.

I realized how much Jesus loved me when I had my children and realized I loved them so much I'd actually give my life for them. That is exactly what Jesus did. He gave His life for you and for me. They nailed Him to a cross and He allowed it because He wanted us to have forgiveness for our sins. The Bible says that He is now sitting at the right hand of His Father, making intercession for us. I'm so glad that through all my hurts I knew Jesus.

The life of a woman is not easy, I know,
I've been to the top and back down,
But I won't look back at yesterday,
I refuse to turn around,
I march forward, day after day,
Victory is *mine*, I shout!
Devil, you get out of here,
Get out, get out, get out!
And when I say that he has to flee,
He no longer has any power over me,
I am God's woman, I am free!

24.

Personality Check

Each one of us should know what we are about. Know what pushes our buttons, know what makes us happy. Most of all, we need to know what we want, and how to work toward that goal.

I decided to do a personality check of myself. It helped me to understand myself better, and why I react to situations the way I do. I am definitely a "type A" personality.

I'll write mine down if you'll write yours!

✳ I have lots of spunk and energy. I can't stand being around slow-moving people.

✳ I'm a little too loud.

✳ I get upset quickly, but it leaves as fast as it came.

✳ I have definite opinions and ideas, and probably talk too much.

✳ I'm a bit of a perfectionist. I fight that part in me.

✳ I cannot sit still for very long. I must stay busy!

✳ I get bored easily.

✳ I love desperately, passionately.

✳ I trust people way too much.

✳ I am capable of hating desperately but have learned to give that part of me to God. I try to always live in forgiveness of those who hurt me.

✳ I hate change, but I need change. When it comes to change, I need a push.

✳ I'm never satisfied with the way I look, the way I sing, etc.

✳ I think I have an inferiority complex. I'm never good enough!

✳ I am extremely loyal to friends.

✳ I forgive easily.

✳ I love fun. I love to laugh. I think funny thoughts.

✳ I love animals, trees, flowers, water. I love nature!

✳ I love clothes, purses, shoes, jewelry, and being thin.

✳ I'm tough! I don't let hardly anything get me down for very long.

✳ I love being taken care of by my husband.

✳ I am *not* a women's libber.

✳ I need to help people to feel fulfilled in life.

✳ My favorite subject to talk about is Jesus, what He has done for me, and what He will do for you if you will just let Him.

✳ I love being a grandmother. (Hi, James and Jonathan! Grandma loves you!)

✳ I love to write. It's one of my great passions in life.

✳ I love lilacs. And puppies and kittens.

Your Personality Checklist

Now it's your turn. Fill in this page. Let your husband or wife read what you write here. It may help them to better understand your needs as a person.

1. _____

2. _____

3. _____

4. _____

5. _____

6. _____

7. _____

8. _____

9. _____

10. _____

25.
Funny Things Happen When You Least Expect It

The other day my girlfriend and I decided to go out for lunch. We sat down in the restaurant, ordered, and were deep into girltalk when the food arrived. All of a sudden, out of nowhere, I began to feel a tickle in my throat. You know the feeling—you know what's coming but you're powerless to stop it. In terror, I looked for the bathroom and just as I got up from my chair it hit me like a bomb! I started to cough uncontrollably. Everyone thought I was choking, so I needed to get out of there fast.

I started toward the restroom as fast as I could when, to my horror, I started wetting my pants. It ran down my legs and onto the floor all the way there. I wanted to die and was afraid I would. To top it off, the male manager came running into the bathroom, and there I was, standing there with my slacks and panties around my knees, trying to stop the flow of urine or sit down on the commode while coughing my guts out, with liquid flowing out of every place it could flow from. Tears were streaming down my face and I felt like I was going to throw up. I guess it was about the most undignified moment of my life. I pray I will never see that man again! But I have a feeling that he and his friends have spent many a merry moment as he's told and retold the story.

Another embarrassing moment occurred recently. Our gardeners in California all spoke Spanish and claimed to speak no English. Now, beautiful, natural-growing shrubs, bushes, and trees are my passion. I am not the manicured-lawn type. I love things to grow wild as God meant for them to grow. I lived in fear of those gardeners! Everywhere I looked I saw their work, and to my eyes, everything cut evenly, trees trimmed to the point of death, and flowers all in a row, are not my idea of beauty.

I don't know how they did it, but the people who lived in our little condo before us had managed to let everything grow as nature intended. I felt our yard was the most beautiful. A huge lemon tree spread its branches out over a little lake; a huge flowering tree stood across the dock from it. Our porch area was completely secluded, surrounded by shrubbery that had gone a little wild in growth.

I got to where I was afraid to leave the house for fear the gardeners would come while I was gone. One day I was at the pool a few houses away, and I heard the noise of their leaf blowers. They were at my house! I jumped out of the pool, and without even thinking about the picture the tabloids would print if someone with a camera saw me, I ran across several lawns screaming at the top of my voice, "You no cutta my bushes, you no cutta my tree! You leava them alone!"

To my dismay, they had already cut the bushes on the side of the house to a neat row. And they had cut my beautiful lemon tree to a pitiful round ball. They were headed for the porch. When they finally saw me pointing to the tree and screaming, "You no cutta my tree," they knew something was definitely wrong. They didn't even have to speak English.

Why do we always think that if we add an "a" after a word that we're speaking Spanish? And that we also must talk very loudly and use extensive sign language?

Anyway, by this time I was not only yelling but tears were streaming down my face. I stood there defiantly as they called someone on their two-way radio. I had no idea what they were saying, but I knew it wasn't good. Before I knew it, a golf cart came humming down the road to our house. And to my horror, there were five people on it, four men and a woman. They had come from the office—they were the "beautification department," or some such thing they only have in Palm Springs, California. Trying to cover my bathing suit as best I could with the small towel I had grabbed, I proceeded to tell them that part of the reason we moved into that particular condo was because of the lush growth of green around it. They must have felt sorry for me standing there in a disheveled, wet, sobbing heap.

They said they would talk it over and get back to me. In the meantime, the yardmen were to go on to another house.

I didn't hear from them and was too embarrassed ever to call. But the next time the yardmen came, the head man was with them. He told me in broken English that they would trim "just a little bit" from now on. They were true to their word, and we all lived happily ever after.

26.

Talk About Embarrassing!

✳ Trying to call my daughter with the television remote . . . and trying to change channels on the television with my cell phone!

✳ Mispronouncing Fudruckers in front of a gang of people.

✳ Talking a hundred miles an hour to your friend in the shopping center and not realizing she's not there until people start looking at you funny. I hate it when that happens. Hey! Stay with me, Melanie! Or at least tell me when you're moving on.

✳ My girlfriend was so excited. She was finally getting an award of excellence for her work as a schoolteacher. The auditorium was packed, and she was a nervous wreck by the time they finally called her name. As she proudly walked toward the podium, her skirt fell off. There she was in her panty hose. We teased her later that she at least had the good taste to match her panty hose to her cream blouse.

Oh, by the way, someone else had to pick up her award for her. She's never come out of the bathroom. . . . Aw, come on out, Tawnsy, *please?*

✳ It was a bitter-cold winter day and snow was falling in Portsmouth, Virginia. We got a call from Pat Robertson saying no one could make it to the TV station. Since we lived so close, could we go do the show? We headed out to the frozen parking lot to get in the car. We no sooner stepped out than a gust of wind sent my wig flying across the parking lot and under another car. I was mortified. I got on my hands and knees in the snow and ice and slithered on my stomach under that car to retrieve my wig. When I finally got to my feet, I looked down—my stockings were torn to shreds and blood was running down my legs. But we made it to the TV station in time and, although I looked a bit worse for the wear, did the show. The show must go on!

✳ It was at the time when all the girls were wearing "beauty marks." Well, I don't like temporary things, so I decided to get my beauty mark tattooed on. I thought it looked really cool. I was playing the organ at our church the next Sunday when a man came up to me and said, "Tammy, that black thing on your face—have you had a doctor check it out? At the stage you have, it could be cancer." I laughed till I cried! I never had the nerve to tell him it was only a tattoo! But ever since, I cover it with makeup. What was I thinking?

✳ I had just started Bible college and was standing with a group of new friends, laughing and talking. One young man started to talk and was stuttering something awful. You could hardly listen to him. Of course, being me, I thought he was joking around. So I started to stutter too. He wasn't joking! I nearly died of embarrassment. The hardest thing I ever did was to face that young man a few days later, full of apologies.

✳ My husband and I were doing our monologue on our TV show. I don't know how we got on the subject, but we were talking about the fact that until I married him I had only had an outdoor bathroom. I piped up without even thinking. "Sure, I only married you for your plumbing!" The studio audience of a thousand people began to laugh and laugh and laugh, and we never did get the show back. The whole hour was filled with uncontrollable laughter. People still remind me of that day years later.

27.

A New You

Have you ever wanted to create a "new you"? I have! A girl can dream, can't she? So let's have a go at it.

This is what I am now:

* Four feet eleven inches tall.

* Small shoulders.

* Short arms that are beginning to sag a bit.

* Short legs.

* Size 5½ feet. (It's hard to buy cute shoes!)

* Pretty hands. (I have my mom's hands. I wear jewelry well!)

❋ Very good skin.

❋ Not an ugly face, but not a beautiful face. It's just a normal, square face.

❋ Pretty blue eyes (after my dad!) and little ears.

❋ Fine, dry hair that could be pretty if I'd leave the scissors alone.

❋ A quick mind. I learn very quickly; I "get" life.

❋ And right at this moment I'm pretty skinny. Thank you, Slim-Fast!

A new me would have the following:

❋ Long, thick, flowing hair. I've always wanted to be able to throw back my hair!

❋ A perfect, dark complexion.

❋ Long legs!

❋ Long feet, with pretty toes.

❋ A tiny waist, like Scarlett in *Gone with the Wind*.

❋ Broad shoulders, so I wouldn't have to wear shoulder pads. Hey, I wonder if there is such a thing as "shoulder implants"? Ha. Ha.

* I'd like to be at least five-foot-three.

* And weigh 105 pounds.

* Long, naturally curly eyelashes.

* Huge eyes.

* Small, tight arms.

* A naturally beautiful face that didn't need makeup. (Now I *am* dreaming!)

Your "New You" List

Now you try. What would the new you be like?

1. _____

2. _____

3. _____

4. _____

5. _____

6. _____

7. _____

8. _____

9. _____

10. _____

28.

How to Lose Weight and Keep It Off

I guess in my lifetime I've lost a hundred pounds over and over again. Gain ten pounds, lose ten pounds; gain seven pounds, lose seven pounds.

When I was a girl I could not gain weight. With ten of us eating in our house, you never got two of anything. Never a second helping! Mom would bake the best cakes you ever put in your mouth. She made a spice cake with peanut-butter frosting. I can still taste that cake. My mouth waters at the thought as I write. I always teased Mom that someday I would write a book and call it *A Second Piece of Cake*. I longed for a second piece of cake, but after everyone had a piece, it was gone. Same with

Mom's fudge, and the cream puffs she made that were so light you couldn't feel any weight until they were filled with real whipping cream. She used to make pie crust rolled out flat on a cookie sheet, cover it in butter, sugar, and cinnamon, and bake it until it was golden brown. It was the best thing I'd ever tasted, and I love it to this day—just plain old pie crust! She'd take more pie crust, cut it in strips, put strawberry jelly in, roll and bake them. Another dessert I could never get enough of.

I was a tiny, tiny little thing. We never went to a doctor, but I was so skinny that my mom called the doctor and asked him what to do to fatten me up a little. He sent her to the drugstore for something that looked and tasted like molasses. Mom knew I loved tomato juice, but we could never afford to buy it. So she spent her last grocery money to get me some tomato juice to put the molasses-like stuff in. I'll never forget drinking it. I don't think it helped too much, though, because when I got married at eighteen I still only weighed eighty-one pounds. That's thin even at my height.

In school everyone called me Squirt. I was so embarrassed when we had to get weighed in front of the class in gym. My legs looked like two little sausages hanging from my body. I remember praying that someday they would touch in the middle like all the other girls'. That's one prayer I wish to God I'd never prayed!

There were never any clothes that would fit me, which was a good thing, because we couldn't afford to buy many clothes. In high school I had a straight black skirt and one full skirt with can-can slips under it. I was so skinny that one day I got off the bus and my huge slips fell right off me onto the ground. Talk about embarrassed! I think I had them safety-pinned at the waist and the pins came undone.

Everything was always too big, but my aunt Gin was good at the sewing machine and would take everything in or up for me. I took a size zero, of which there was no such thing in those days.

I loved pretty blouses and was able to buy them for ten cents at the Salvation Army store. My favorite one was paisley. To me it was the most beautiful blouse in the world. I always felt pretty when I wore that blouse.

One day on the way home from school I stopped at the Salvation Army store, where they were having a sale on bras. I was fourteen and was embarrassed that all the other girls wore bras and I'd never even tried one on. I picked out a pretty pink one. I couldn't wait to get home, run up to my room, and put it on. My heart was racing! By stuffing it with Kleenex, I finally got it to look right. I went downstairs to help Mom set the table for supper and felt like Marilyn Monroe. No one seemed to notice, not even Mom, but I finally felt like a woman. And high school was never the same after that!

I started gaining weight after I got married. I could finally have that second piece of cake. It wasn't Mom's cake, but it was cake. I went from eighty-one pounds to about a hundred pounds and stayed that way until I had my first baby. During my pregnancy I gained about twenty-five pounds, and it just would not move. For the first time in my life I learned what it meant to diet. And I dieted and dieted in vain. I'd lose a couple of pounds and put them back on. I see myself in some of the old TV footage and cannot believe how heavy I got. My legs more than touched in the middle—they rubbed together.

More recently, when I moved from California, where I had lived for seven years, back to Charlotte, I noticed two distinct differences in the people. One was people speaking openly about God. In California, I don't remember ever hearing people talking about God or church or praying or miracles while they were shopping. In the Carolinas, it's rather a way of life. No one thinks anything of it. To me it's so refreshing to see ' people who are not ashamed of the Gospel of Jesus Christ and who talk about Him openly.

The second thing I noticed is how pretty the ladies of the Carolinas are. In Palm Springs, they went from one extreme to the other. Either they had facelifts and were dressed to the nines, or they were running around in tennis shoes and shorts paying not much attention to *what* they looked like.

The Carolina ladies are so round and pretty. I don't like hugging bones! I like a little padding on those bones. They're curvy. In many cases I'd say technically they're about thirty pounds overweight. They dress in suits or pantsuits or slacks with sweaters or blouses, always striving to look as nice as they can. I love the way they look. I don't think there's anything wrong with a few extra pounds, if those pounds don't interfere with your health. I feel that if you eat normally, your body will automatically stay a certain weight, whether it's a few pounds over or under. I have seen so many of my friends lose those thirty pounds, and then when they start eating normally again—normal being the amount of food that satisfies you, where you don't feel that you are denying yourself—they go right back to the weight they were before.

Part of that may be habit. Habits of snacking, or a love for certain kinds of fattening foods. But if you love 'em before you started losing weight, you're still going to love 'em after you've lost the weight. Therein lies the problem!

I think heredity and body shape both figure into weight loss. They make it harder for some, easier for others. Look at Mom and Grandma! To my way of thinking, that's the reason you gain and lose and gain and lose the same weight over and over and over. So I think you either get comfortable with being a few pounds overweight, or you must be willing to change what you eat, and how much of it. A bite or two of anything, no matter how filled with fat, is not going to hurt you or put on weight. But can you stop eating a chocolate delight topped with whipped cream after just two bites? Hummmmm . . . probably not, if you're used to eating an entire dessert.

The very word "diet" gets me to thinking sacrifice. Self-denial. The word does not evoke excitement. If I eat what I want and love, I will stay about twenty-five pounds overweight. But I just did lose those extra twenty-five pounds about six months ago. I feel great, I have a wonderful figure and love the way I look in my new, smaller clothes. My square face looks thinner, which I love, and I receive compliments every day— yes, every day! "Oh, you're so tiny. I didn't realize you were so tiny!" I just smile and say thank you. People will even say silly things like, "Hey, your boobs look bigger—have you done something?" When you lose twenty-five pounds your waist gets smaller, therefore your boobs look bigger, ladies. That's a good thing, I think!

I am enjoying being able to wear belts again. Big belts used to be my trademark. But it got to where when I gained weight my waist was big, my boobs were big, and there was no room left in-between for a belt! So bringing down the middle was a major victory for me.

You might ask me what foods I have a hard time with now. Well, I love Wendy's hamburgers, pizza of any kind, cake, pie, and candy of any kind. I think my downfall is always too many sweets too often. Anything chocolate! I never have overeaten on just plain old food, but sweets are a different story. Those desserts will do it every time. I could have dessert after every meal—or *before* every meal. Yes, before. My friends have always teased me about sitting down in a restaurant and ordering dessert first. I laughingly tell them I have my priorities straight: If I don't eat it before, I might not get it at all. So I'd eat a big piece of pumpkin pie with extra whipped cream before I even got my food. I guess that's the reason I never ate much of my actual food! The stuff that's good for you, likes vegetables. Hey, what is a vegetable? Isn't pumpkin a vegetable?

I also have a love for fried foods, especially french fries. With lots of ketchup. And fried chicken. *All* preachers love fried chicken. If we didn't, we'd starve to death. Every time someone asks a preacher for dinner, you can count on fried chicken.

I often think of a fact I read some years ago that startled me. It was that if you eat just one extra cookie a week, it can mean a five-pound weight gain by the end of the year. And most people in fact gain on an average of five pounds per year. That's right in my case. When I'm 139 pounds, if I wear black and stay away from belts, wear my hair high, and wear big shoulder pads and high heels, I don't look *that* heavy. I gain weight all over so I don't look misshapen. So I can actually carry it off pretty well. But I hate to walk around holding my stomach in all the time, wishing I were thinner and could look good in something besides black.

Now here is a fact for you older ladies: When you're heavier, your face looks younger! The bigger you blow up a balloon, the fewer wrinkles you will have. When I lost weight it accentuated lines I didn't know I had. Yuck! You get thin and the skin has to go somewhere! Why is it, I'd like to know, that when you get older your skin gets too big for your body? Hmmmm. Do your bones shrink, maybe? All I know is that I now have extra skin in places that I can't believe!

So those few extra pounds are a matter of choice. Which look do you like better? Thin and looking great in your clothes, or a little heavier with a younger face? I heard someone say, and I think they're right, that after fifty you sacrifice either your face or your figure.

Well, anyway, how did I lose my twenty-five pounds? I heard on TV about a drink that was filled with vitamins and also good for weight loss. I was more concerned with the vitamins, which I felt my body might be lacking, than the weight loss. I bought some—chocolate, of course—and began drinking two "shakes" a day, and eating one regular meal. It worked fantastically. Before this, I had to take a nap every day at about three in the afternoon. I'd just lose my energy. I'd lie down for an hour, and after that I could go until midnight. It was just that slump during the day. Now I had so much wonderful energy— no afternoon downtime. I actually started making my bed every day, since I wasn't getting back into it in the middle of the afternoon.

But I also noticed something else: I wasn't craving sweets. I was actually craving apples, bananas, and vegetables! I'd never craved an *apple* in my life, and certainly not vegetables.

I had another wonderful surprise: In three weeks, I'd lost eighteen pounds. I was ecstatic. I cut the drink back to once a day, with two regular meals. I now drink it for breakfast only, a meal I have never eaten anyway. I eat all I want for lunch, and at night I usually eat cereal and a bagel. If we go out to eat, I'll eat a naked potato, only a little salt on it, a salad with the dressing on the side, and a piece of meat, which I end up taking most of home in a doggie bag for my two little dogs. Honest! Muffin and Tuppins *do* get the meat!

I actually have learned I can eat a little of anything I want. It's all portion control. So I do not consider myself to be on a diet. I will always drink the drink, and it will probably always be chocolate. I watch my fat grams. I automatically look for the fat-gram count on everything I put in my mouth. If it's not worth the fat grams, I just don't eat it. If it is, then I do eat it. Like pumpkin pie. That's always worth the fat grams.

I do not feel deprived. I eat four or five french fries when I want them, and I still get my share of sweets; the difference is I don't crave them like I used to.

Oh, by the way, the company that makes the diet drink also makes candy bars, and they're delicious. They have one that tastes exactly like Butterfingers, my favorite candy bar. We keep them in the house all the time, as my husband loves them too.

The rewards of losing the weight are greater than the rewards of overeating. I weigh myself every day. I wear clothes that are tight around the waist, not elastic, which reminds me not to overeat. I drink a lot of liquids. And I walk a lot. I'll park the car as far away from the store as possible, and it forces me to walk. Then, no matter how tired I am when I'm finished, I still have to walk back to the car. I never try to find a parking place close by—even in the rain. I'm not sugar, I won't melt. At least that's what my mom always told me.

I also bought a treadmill . . . but I don't use it very often. At least I know it's there. My sweet husband mounted a small TV on the wall in front of the treadmill so I wouldn't have to be bored when using it. I think he really loves my weight loss. But why not? He still weighs the same as he did in high school. He's a golfer and exercises every day.

I have also found out that stairs are a good thing. I cannot believe what twenty-five fewer pounds did for me when it comes to walking upstairs. I hated those stairs. Now I gleefully run up the stairs, just because I can. And I don't even get winded. Try carrying twenty-five extra pounds up the stairs sometime and feel the difference.

I feel sexier with less weight. When I was heavier, I always kept my body tan. I have a tanning machine I would use faithfully. I didn't care if it was good for my skin or not. I just felt that dark fat looks better than white fat. Now I hardly ever think of tanning, except in the summer when I put self-tanner on my feet and legs. But that's so the veins don't show. Where in the world did *they* come from? Whoever called after fifty the golden years was out of their mind! I can't even look like *silver,* much less gold!

Will I keep the weight off? I hope so! I like how I feel now and how I look in clothes. I like my energy level, and I haven't found any food that I cannot live without. When I weigh the advantages against the disadvantages, I feel like staying slimmer outweighs eating anything I want whenever I want. Plus, I've invested too much in new clothes! My husband would kill me! And I gave away my heavier clothes, which were size ten and twelve. I now wear a size four or six petite on the bottom and have gone from a large to medium and sometimes even a small on top, depending on how the garment is made.

Again—if you enjoy the weight you are and if it's not affecting your health, enjoy it. "Don't worry, be happy!" If you don't, you *can* do something about it. You can do anything if you want to badly enough. And if you stick with it long enough, it will become a habit, not a chore.

Oh, I forgot another thing that may help: Eat only half of what you put on your plate. Especially in a restaurant. Remember, they put enough on a plate for a large man. If you only eat half of what you usually eat, you won't *have* to lose weight. And don't forget, my friend: Walk! Walk! Walk! It's good for you!

To Diet Or Not to Diet

Here are some tips:

* Eat only half of what's on your plate. Take the rest home in a doggie bag, for you or the doggie in your life!

* Learn to eat things naked! Now, that doesn't mean to eat without any clothes on, although that might be a good idea! Ha! It simply means not to add the sour cream and bacon bits and butter to that baked potato. And use less gravy and sauce.

* Try counting fat grams and calories. Find out how many fat grams and calories your body needs. You'll be surprised at how fast they add up. And you'll be surprised how few fat grams one can live on.

* If it's not absolutely fantastic, delicious, delectable, etc., forget it. It's not worth it. You'll regret later putting things in your tummy that you didn't even really enjoy eating.

* One day a week I treat myself to all the dessert I can eat. That works for me, and I usually eat a lot less than I thought I would.

* Just because "everyone else is doing it" doesn't make it right for you. *(continued)*

To Diet Or Not to Diet *(cont'd)*

✳ If you can, walk! Walk! Walk! Park at the back of the parking lot if it's safe, not at the front.

✳ Tan fat looks better than white fat—Ooops! Didn't mean to put that one in.

✳ Wear good supportive undergarments. Sagging anything is *not a pretty sight!* I went to a show one time where all the performers were over sixty. I was sitting about halfway back in the theater, and eighty-year-old women had bodies that looked better than mine. I was ready to just shoot myself. What in the world were they doing looking that good, in bathing suits no less, at their age?

After the show, the performers stood at the back of the theater shaking hands. As I shook this eighty-year-old lady's hand, I sighed with relief! She had a body stocking on from her neck to the bottom of her feet. And she was wearing spandex. From this I learned one thing that works no matter how old or what size you are. It's all illusion! But that's not bad—I'll take illusion if I have to.

✳ Don't wear shorts without panty hose if you're overweight. If you do, wear the longer shorts. There's nothing that looks worse than a heavy person in shorts with no support. And be sure and check yourself in a mirror from the *back* as well as the front. Some things that look great from the front look awful from the back or the side.

✳ If fat is hanging out above and below your bra, it's too tight, honey! Think again!

✳ Make sure you have at least one full-length mirror in your house. You can buy them cheap at Kmart or Wal-Mart. Hang it where you have room enough to stand back so you can actually see your entire body, including your feet.

✳ Many people who are overweight tend to think that tight clothes make them look smaller. That's not true—it's exactly the opposite. When I'm heavier, I wear loose-fitting clothes that flow around me. And I wear all one color, top and bottom. That includes shoes. It's slimming. Now that I am thinner, I still have a hard time wearing anything too fitted, because I still think I'm heavier. But thinner people look smaller in fitted clothes, I have found.

✳ I love jackets. They cover a multitude of sins. One time I took off my jacket, and Jim Bullock said to me, "Tam, why don't you ever let your figure show? You have a great shape!" That now gives me courage not to always wear a jacket with everything.

✳ You don't have to be a fashion hound. If the fashion that's in does not look good on you, *don't go there.* I worry very little about fashion—it changes so quickly. That's the way the fashion industry keeps making its money. They change the fashion from long to short, from your tummy showing to everything covered. *(continued)*

To Diet Or Not to Diet *(cont'd)*

(Oh, by the way, showing your tummy, no matter how good it looks, is for the very young.) I do like to keep up with the current color trends. This year I added camel to my wardrobe. But again, if it doesn't look good on *you*, then wear the style and the colors that make you feel special.

✳ Clothes have a lot to do with how we feel about ourselves. I feel totally different in pants than I do in a skirt. I even act differently. I'm more ladylike in a skirt. I feel more feminine. So what you wear really does matter. And you don't have to have a lot of money to look great.

✳ Ladies, don't forget to add a little lipstick to complete the picture. Lipstick shows you care.

29.

Colors

Never underestimate the power of a little red dress!
An old man once told me that.

I always feel confident in red. I don't know why. They say red is a power color. There are times I just have to wear red, and then I'll go for months when I don't even *like* the color red. When I used to go to Rochester, Minnesota, to visit Jim in prison, if I didn't have something red with me I'd have to go buy something. The red gave me courage, it seemed.

They say colors can really affect people. I believe it. Blue actually makes me feel blue. I *never* wear blue because of that, even though my eyes are deep blue. And I hardly ever wear anything pastel, except lavender, which makes me feel good about myself.

I prefer deep, bright colors. But then what do I know? Some say my favorite color isn't really a color at all: I *love* black. If I could choose one outfit to wear for the rest of my life, it would be a black jumpsuit. If you don't feel good in black, chocolate brown is a great neutral color. I also love white, but when I wear a white blouse I tend to get makeup on it and I hate that. I have literally scrubbed my neck till it was raw and still found traces of makeup on the collar of a white blouse. (There must be a joke in there somewhere. I'm sure Comedy Central could find one.)

As for colors in my house, I love deep green tones and burgundy tones. Both add richness to any room. I also like celery green. I wouldn't wear celery green, but, I think it makes a beautiful room. And it has a calming effect.

I love to sleep in pink. Everything I buy to feel cozy in is pink. My nightgown is pink, my bathrobe is pink. Pink to me is relaxing. I very seldom wear pink during the day, unless it's a bright, shocking pink. I think colors are important to energy levels and to relaxation. For instance, I can't wear orange or yellow, or certain shades of green.

I don't know what dictates the colors we like or don't. I used to think it was either skin tone, eye color, or hair color. Ultimately, that is what should dictate the colors we wear, if we want to make a fashion statement. For instance, I think blondes look better in pastels because they're very feminine, while redheads look great in electric blue, golds, browns, greens, and camel colors. People with dark brown or black hair can wear just about any color.

I love blond hair, but I feel washed out as a blonde. I had my hair bright red for years. I feel more feminine in blond hair, more daring and fun in red hair, and just normal in brown hair. Black hair is striking and "pops," but very few people can wear jet-black hair and look good in it. I look totally different in black hair. I can wear it because I have dark skin and these deep blue eyes. But it feels harsh to me, so I always end up putting blond streaks in it.

I can wear almost any color, for which I am thankful, since I get bored easily. Poor Roe never knows what I'm going to look

I love hats and belts and scarves and purses,
Jewelry, makeup and shoes,
And sitting around with my girlfriends,
Listening to all the news,
Who's having a baby or getting a tuck,
Or adding to their hair.
Our poor husbands, sometimes they must feel
Like they aren't even there.

like when he gets home. A wild redhead, a sexy blonde, or a dark brunette. I have wigs in every one of those colors. Right now, as I write this, my hair is short and dark brown with blond frosting on just the top.

I also have an opinion on gold versus silver jewelry. I think some people look better in gold. Gold looks marvelous on dark skin. I think silver looks great on lighter skin. However, I wear much more silver than gold—unless I'm wearing both, which I often do. One thing about silver jewelry: it's not as expensive as gold, so you can own a lot more of it! And I love big, bulky jewelry, so silver fills the bill for me. Or should I say fits my budget. Pearls look great on skin of any color, and they can be worn with anything from blue jeans to evening clothes. As can diamonds!

I *hate* sneakers and tennis shoes. It seems we've become obsessed with them. My aunt Gin used to tell me, "It takes pains to be beautiful." Well, you don't have to worry about being beautiful in sneakers. I own one pair—but they're high-heel sneakers! In my opinion, unless you have a medical problem with your feet or back, sneakers should be worn only for playing sports or exercising. Shoes make or break an outfit. You may have on a beautiful outfit and jewelry, but if you wear the wrong shoes with it, it ruins the effect. To me, people who only wear sneakers or tennis shoes are saying, "I don't care what I look like." That's not *wrong;* everyone has his or her own taste. But I miss the days when dressing was an art and when people actually cared. I think when you're dressed well you feel better about yourself and have better self-esteem. Clothes matter. When I wear jeans I automatically sit differently, and it's not feminine.

I think it's so frustrating to go to a dressy event and half the people are wearing clothes that look like they just didn't bother or didn't care. I guess that's why I love black so much. It can go anywhere at any time and look good. Even black jeans and a black t-shirt manage to look great.

If you want to feel better about yourself, clothes are a good place to start, and they don't have to be expensive. I've seen and bought beautiful, classy pieces at the Goodwill. My daughter just bought a pair of gorgeous designer shoes there for $3. I shop thrift shops all the time. I love the money I save and feel great about the bargains I get. You don't have to have a lot of money to look good. You just have to care.

30.

Dress Rich on a Budget

You don't have to be rich to look rich. You don't have to shop at Saks Fifth Avenue to look like Saks Fifth Avenue.

This is what I have done for years: I get catalogs from all the higher-priced stores. I see what the models are wearing and figure out what's in for this year. Then I start to shop—at T.J. Maxx, Marshalls, Steinmart, Value City, Burlington Coat Factory, and every other little fun store I can find. Even Kmart and Target have wonderful copies of the expensive stuff.

One year I found a pair of gold high heels in the Saks catalog. I wanted those shoes so bad I could hardly stand it. They were all little straps that wound halfway up your leg. But I couldn't pay $350 for a pair of shoes. But then I found the same shoes in leather-looking plastic for $20. I was so excited

I bought two pair! I still wear them and still get compliments on them.

The other day I saw a skirt I had to have in an expensive store. I *sure* wasn't going to pay $100 for a straight little cotton skirt, so I kept shopping. I walked into this really inexpensive little hole-in-the-wall and, lo and behold, there was a whole rack of these skirts, looking *exactly* like the one I wanted, for $10, in every color. I bought white and black and camel. No one would ever have guessed!

Just the other day at Burlington Coat Factory I found a long leather (look-alike) coat. I shuddered to think what the price on this awesome coat was going to be. But heck, I tried it on anyway. I had the shock of my life! It was $16.98. I not only bought the long coat but also the matching jacket for $14.98. They both look and feel like the real thing—I challenge anyone to tell the difference. I bought a black purse to match. What a truly great-looking outfit. Shabby chic!

That same day I saw a pair of camel-colored boots I had to have. But they were $150, so I went shopping again. I found the same look, same color at Pic 'n Pay for guess how much—$12! And they look fantastic. Got the matching purse for about the same.

I've found that places like T.J. Maxx and Marshalls and Value City sell exactly the same things the expensive department stores do, but the designer tags have either been removed or covered by a black marker or cut in half. That doesn't matter to me; I don't care which designer name is in a place no one but me ever sees. When was the last time someone said to you, "Can I see the tag on that blouse you're wearing?" So keep your tag to yourself and enjoy!

I do the same thing with purses. They make great copies of

everything these days. They sell them at flea markets and on the streets of New York City. They also have "purse parties" where they sell copies. And sometimes you can buy the real thing at resale shops for less than half the price of the original. I've bought a couple of Louis Vuitton purses that way. To make sure you're paying for the genuine item, look under the tag inside the purse. If it's genuine, there'll be an ID number under there.

A few days ago I picked up the softest camel-colored jacket I'd ever touched. I wrapped myself in it and realized it was reversible. And it was 100 percent cashmere! The price: $39.99. It's now hanging in my closet waiting for a cold spell. Buying out of season, if you can afford to and can wait to wear it, can bring you some wonderful bargains. That coat would have cost me $200 or more in a designer store. I'll get a lot of wear out of that jacket and feel great in it too. And no one (except you) needs to know what I paid for it.

You can do the same with jewelry and diamonds. All my "diamonds" come from T.J. Maxx. They have fantastic cubic zirconium jewelry set in 14K gold. Keep them clean and no one will ever know. Only a jeweler, and he has to look at them through a loop. If you can't afford to buy cubics set in 14K gold, get them in silver—it looks like white gold, and silver shows off a stone and makes it look bigger.

My husband asked the other day,
"Honey, where did the closet space go?
Can't you leave *some* room for me?
I live in this house too, you know."

Well, I blame that problem on Marshalls, also on T.J. Maxx,
For when they put their clothes on sale, I have a shopping
    attack.
I always drive home proudly,
My trunk filled with bargains I've found,
Just think of all the money I've saved, because I shopped
    around.

But as I drive up I see *his* car—
He's come home early today.
I walk in the house empty-handed; he says, "Hello, Tammy
    Faye."
I wait until he goes to the den
And turns the TV on ball,
Then I run to the car, get all my stuff, and sneak it down
    the hall.

What he don't know won't hurt me I say,
I'll just show him my bargains some other day,
They'll be *older* that way.
"New? This old thing? I've had it awhile,"
I say as I sashay by,
But I know I'm not fooling him one little bit,
There's a twinkle in his eye!

31.

Traveling Light

Have you ever gone to the airport and almost missed your plane because the woman in front of you had so many bags to check? Then when you got on the plane she blocked the aisle for several minutes trying to shove things into the overhead bin. You went to sit down and could hardly get by for the things on the floor that were supposed to be under the seat in front of her.

Well, that has happened to me, and I vowed never to carry that much stuff on a plane, ever. (It's a little different now as they limit the number of bags you can carry on anyway.)

I have traveled all over the world and have done so with a relatively small amount of luggage. And you can, too, if you will learn to pack smart.

First of all, I always travel with one basic color. My color is black. It goes with everything, you can dress it up or down, it's suitable for every occasion, and my black clothes do not wrinkle. *(Do not wear linen.)* I start with black pants, add a colorful blouse or light sweater, and finish with a matching black jacket. It can get chilly on the plane, so sleeves help. I finish with black or plastic see-through shoes (a must-have in my wardrobe). Plastic shoes go with anything and give your leg a long look. I carry with me a black, see-through backpack. I found a great one at Target. In it I carry my CD player, my good jewelry, snacks for the plane, magazines, and a small purse with my wallet, makeup, etc.

When I pack my suitcases, everything coordinates with everything else. Try to bring along accessories; you'd be surprised how they change your look in a minute. Scarves can work miracles on a trip. And they add color and punch to your base color. I take an animal-print scarf (leopard or zebra) and a red scarf, a white scarf, and fun jewelry to match. Accessories add some punch. And I *love* punch. They make clothes POP!

Belts are fun. And they give clothes a punch. Vests are fun too. They pack light and can be as funky as you like, or look very businesslike.

You cannot imagine how many changes of clothes you can get in a suitcase if you use this method of packing. And it's so funny, people never even realize that you're basically wearing the same black suit.

I always take my black skirt so that if I need one I have one. And I carry a black sweater so that I can wear the sweater and pants or skirt and it makes it look like a dress or pantsuit. Add a belt or a scarf and bingo—well dressed for the day. In the winter, I also take along a pair of black boots.

I like to carry my basic hanging clothes with me on the plane. Put dry-cleaning bags over them and then your garment bag, and they're guaranteed not to wrinkle. I put ribbons on my hanging bag (I've had a bag taken and never got it back); you can spot your ribbons immediately. I also put ribbons on my luggage, making it quick to spot. And someone else isn't as likely to walk off with your stuff. I also put my name and address and phone number inside the suitcase I carry.

If you're going to be gone for a long time, make sure you bring wash-and-wear clothing. I don't care if they do make fun of polyester. It's wash-and-wear and never wrinkles. I love it.

I always bring a wig, ladies. Traveling to different humidity zones can wreak havoc with the best hairdo. Wigs don't mind humidity, or rain. You just shake them out and put them back on, and your hair always looks great. Get the light wigs. They have them so light you don't know you have them on your head. And *pin them on* with long bobby pins. I make a little pin curl and fasten the bobby pin along with the wig to that. Then in case of wind you'll feel secure. Chasing a bouncing wig across the parking lot is a little embarrassing. Just as you go to grab it, it gets away again.

Take a bigger suitcase than you actually need—for shopping. They have wheels now, so they are easily managed.

And if you *must* wear jeans and tennis shoes, at least wear something great on top, like a matching jeans jacket.

32.

Fun with Nail Polish

Nail polish can be used for far more than polishing your nails, girls! I have had fun with polish for years, and now that polish comes in so many more colors—yellow, black, green, lavender, purple—and it sparkles and glows, there is no end to what you can do with it!

1. Paint your tired eyeglass frames and have a new pair of glasses! I have red ones, pink ones, black ones, and, oh yes, lavender glasses!

2. Repair a scratch on your shoe.

3. Paint the heels of your shoes a different color from the shoe.

4. I needed a lavender pair of shoes to match a dress. I painted a pair of white strappy sandals with lavender polish matched exactly to the dress.

5. Paint jewelry! Make it any color you want with nail polish. One of my favorite and most complimented pieces is a clear stone I painted with lavender nail polish. (I just painted the bottom of the stone so the color showed through.) It's beautiful!

6. My husband almost died when I painted a deep scratch on the car with nail polish I mixed to exactly the color of the car. Well, almost exactly . . . but it looks a whole lot better than a bare scratch!

7. Create a special picture frame.

8. Use letterforms and personalize the tops of your makeup bottles.

9. Polish now comes in gold and silver. Cover that ring band that has turned.

10. Nail polish works great on purses as a trim.

11. Liven up a pair of tennis shoes.

12. Make your own personalized stationery. Your friends will love it!

13. Change the color of the buttons on a blouse (just don't be sloppy and get the polish on your clothes!).

14. Back to jewelry. Someone gave me a beautiful piece of jewelry, but it was a color I don't wear. Black nail polish fixed that fast! Now I wear it all the time. And

if I get tired of black I could just paint it again. Maybe red.

15. I have even painted the tops of my keys different colors—red for the house key, pink for the mailbox, etc. Works great!

Now be creative and come up with a few ideas of your own.

33.

Make Your Own Jewelry

To make fun jewelry, all you need is some old jewelry or pierced or clip earring backs (you can find them at any craft store, like Michael's) and some E6000 Glue—it glues anything to anything! I have made earrings, rings, pins, hair clips—you name it! And you can make your own creations too!

I took those new one-dollar coins and made the most beautiful earrings. I glued them to clip-on backs because they are a little heavy. I also made a matching ring. I just took an old flat ring and glued the coin on top of it. It's one of my favorites. This is a fun, easy, and inexpensive project (you can even use pennies!). Just cover the coin with a little clear nail polish to keep it looking bright and new.

I use clear nail polish a lot. If you are allergic to the gold on your ring, just brush clear nail polish over the inside of the band. This will keep your finger from turning black. (Don't laugh! 14K gold turns my finger black at certain times of the year. I don't know why.) Clear nail polish also works on inexpensive jewelry with stones. Just one coat will keep the stones from falling out.

Another favorite piece of mine is a ring I made with a beautiful coin surrounded by little diamonds. It was meant to be worn around the neck on a chain, but I never wore it. So I took a pair of clippers and snipped off the bail of the pendant (that's the hanger thing that you put the chain through) and glued the coin to another flat ring that I didn't wear. It is gorgeous! There is a small spot where I cut off the bail that you can see if you look real hard, but a jeweler could buff it right out. It's not important to me. I move my hands so fast when I'm talking no one could ever see it!

I take earrings that I no longer wear and make all kinds of things out of them. I glue them onto plain bracelets, purses, picture frames, and shoes. I glue them to just about anything. It's so much fun to recycle, and you'll feel so proud of your accomplishment. *I made it myself!*

Old jewelry can be recycled in so many wonderful ways. I buy interesting junk jewelry at flea markets. They often have baskets full of it for fifty cents or a dollar. It's fun to dig through them . . . you never know what treasures you'll find. If you see inexpensive flat rings that you don't like, buy them anyway and save them for your next ring creation. They must be flat or the glue will not hold your item securely.

Old jewelry can turn a jean jacket or a pair of plain jeans into a designer-looking piece of clothing. I once saw some horribly expensive shoes that had stones all over the heels. They looked like diamonds. So I went to the craft store, got a couple of bags of shiny little stones, got myself eyebrow tweezers and some

E6000 glue, and went to work on my high-heel shoes. They turned out gorgeous! And they looked just like the expensive ones! If you have the patience and a little time, you can create exclusive, beautiful things. Look in magazines for ideas. See what is "in" and try to create the look yourself.

34.

Facelifts and Wigs: Should You?

In Palm Springs, most of the society women look alike. They are many shades of blond, and their faces have been pulled in a variety of ways by their plastic surgeons.

Now, it's quite easy to tell who did what to whom in high society. Some look as if they are in perpetual surprise. These are the ladies who have had a brow lift. Their eyebrows are skimming their hairline.

Then there are the ladies who look as if they got caught in a strong wind. Their faces are pulled tightly to the ears. In some of these facelifts, the nose has gone with it and now covers more of the face than it should.

Then there are the ladies who have been pulled so tightly in an upward motion that their top lip no longer moves when they speak. And those who have had the bottom lip made so large that they look like Goldie Hawn's character in *First Wives Club*. When you look at them, all you see is that *big lip*. It's supposed to look sexy, but to me it just looks like they've been punched in the mouth. It looks like their lips *hurt*. Sorry, ladies. It's just my opinion.

Then there are the ladies who have had their eyes done so tightly that they can no longer close them all the way and have to use artificial tears to keep their eyes moistened. That happened to my girlfriend. She carries that bottle with her everywhere she goes.

Then there are the facial implants. I was fascinated to find out all the kinds of face implants that are available to whoever can afford them. You can get new cheekbones, new chins . . . well, I guess that's all I know about, because my girlfriend got both.

Did you know that they could cut off ears that stick out and put them back on so they lie flat?

Now, I think plastic surgery's a good thing if it helps a person feel better about themselves. But ladies and gentlemen, check out your doctor. Make sure he or she is licensed to do plastic surgery. And make sure you actually see for yourself some of the work they've done on patients, not just in pictures. Plastic-surgery patients never mind showing off their doctor's work.

It's not that I don't understand the why's of plastic surgery. And it's not that I don't like it when it's done well—like Dixie Carter, of *Designing Women*. She looks fantastic! And she's the first to admit that she loved her new look. Not that it matters to anyone, but I like it too.

But there are some ladies on television who, after they had their faces done, I honestly did not recognize. Only by their voices can I figure out who they are. I could name a few of them, but that wouldn't be nice, so I'll leave it there. Some of them are forever changed for the better; they look refreshed and prettier, like Phyllis Diller. I love her, by the way. And she's beautiful both inside and out. Then there are those I feel should have left well enough alone, as my grandma Fairchild used to say. Some look younger at sixty-five or seventy than they did at thirty. To me that's just strange. I don't mind looking younger, but forty years? I don't think so. And you notice I said "younger," not "more beautiful." And no matter how young and beautiful the face, the aging process doesn't stop. The problem there is that people expect you to act as young as you look. Think about that! Again, that's just my opinion. I'm sure people could care less what I think.

Will I ever have a facelift? Probably. It depends on how far down my jowls fall! Have I had anything done? Yes. I have had liposuction. I have the same figure as my mom, my grandmother, and my aunts—that little round figure. We're all under five feet tall, so you gain a pound and it looks like five. The problem with liposuction is that my once smooth skin is not so smooth anymore. I can live with that, as only my husband sees me without clothes. And it does make a person look better in their clothes. That's what everyone else sees. But if you don't want uneven skin, don't get liposuction.

Would I do it again? Yes, in a minute.

I think almost every woman should own a wig. It makes every day a good hair day. And if you feel good about the way you look, you feel better about everything else.

I keep my hair very short. I have always cut my own hair, colored my own hair, and given myself permanents. That's the reason I wear wigs! Roe likes my own hair better than the wigs,

Do I need a facelift, let me look and see,
Are those sagging jowls looking back at me?
Are my eyes looking smaller?
What are those lines around my mouth?
Then I look down at my body and everything is
    heading south!
Once I start I can't stop, one thing leads to another,
I guess I'll just have to be content,
I've become my MOTHER!

but my wigs are kind of like my security blanket. I think every woman should have at least one wig for emergencies. How many times has your husband asked you to go somewhere with him and you don't want to go because you're having a bad hair day? And I don't know about you, but when my hair looks bad I feel bad all over. Nothing you wear looks good if your hair doesn't look good.

Buying a wig can be a little frustrating, but you'll get the hang of it if you just keep trying. Go to a wig store and just start trying them on. Be adventurous! Try on different styles, different colors, and different lengths. They'll style them on you if you wish, even cut them for you. Also try on a wig before you make a drastic change in your own hair. It may save you some mistakes.

The first thing I do with a wig is have it thinned. Every wig I have ever had on my head has too much hair. That's what makes them look "wiggy." A wig should never look perfect either. That also makes it look wiggy. I don't like perfect hair. I think hair should look fun—yes, even if you're older. The right wig can take years off your appearance. I will *never* allow myself to go gray. I think gray ages the face. If you feel comfortable in gray, then it's your head, but *please* wear at least lipstick so you don't look washed out.

A wig is both functional and fun. And yes, it will stay on (unless you're in a windy parking lot), and no, they aren't heavy anymore. I wear one almost all the time and don't even realize I have one on my head. I can't feel it anymore. I like to go with the current color of my own hair when buying a wig, because I like to pull my own hair out in front and blend it with the wig hair. It's foolproof.

Keep your wig clean. I wash my wigs every week or two when I am wearing them every day. The ones I wear just occasionally I wash only when needed. They have wig shampoo, but I use any kind. If you buy a human-hair wig, you'll have to curl it and so on just as you would your own hair. And I try to keep my wigs on a wig head. However, if you don't have enough room to have wig heads sitting around, just stuff the wig with tissue paper and store it in a closet. It will be fine.

How long does a wig last? I've had them last a couple of years, but then others I've had turned fuzzy in six months. I think it depends on how well you take care of them. Big point: Keep them away from hot ovens. The heat makes them frizzy.

How much should you pay for a wig? I pay anywhere from $30 to $150. They seem to last about the same length of time. A human-hair wig can cost $400 or more. I like the $30 wigs just as well as the expensive ones, as long as the color is right. You can order them through wig catalogs. It might take a few orders, and you may have to send them back a few times, but when you finally get the perfect one it's worth the trouble.

I finally figured out that if you order wig swatches (they're free), you won't make as many color mistakes. The color charts in the catalog are never anywhere near the color you end up with. I find the colors are lighter on the color charts than they are in person.

So go for it, gals! And the next time you get caught in the rain, just take your hair off, shake it, and put it back on. You'll look like you just got out of the beauty parlor!

Golden Years

A little nip here and a little tuck there,
Now I can wear that sexy underwear,
Suck it out here and put it up there,
We're living in a day when ugly is rare.

I walked into the hospital a little bit glazed,
I'd worried about this surgery for days and days,
I sure hated to spend so much money on me,
But I was putting it out where everyone could see.

I wanted my eyes done and also my nose,
I needed those jowls done, my chin line now shows,
I needed my boobs pulled up a bit,
And my waist tucked in so I could see my hips,
My tummy done so I could see my feet,
Then I needed hormones so I could stand the heat.

They call these the golden years,
I sure don't get that,
All I want is chocolate, all I get is fat!
Bones now ache I didn't know I had,
And they say getting old isn't so bad.
If it wasn't for Vicks, green salve, and Deep Heat,
I'd be stuck in my bed,
Not walking on my feet.

So, my dear young friends, enjoy your youth,
Your energy and your smooth skin,
Because when it's gone, no matter what they say,
You won't get it back again.
Oh, you can do all the things mentioned above,
And sure, it will help now and then,
But the time always comes, no matter what they say,
You'll have to do it all over again.
So, my advice is don't ever start,
What's important is in your heart!

35.

Tammy's Makeup Tips

I have never been able to figure out why people have taken my makeup so seriously. It baffles me!

First of all, makeup is not the unpardonable sin! In fact, it's not a sin at all. I don't think God really cares about little colored pencils, tubes with colored sticks in them, little containers that hold colored dust, skin-colored liquid in a bottle, or little pieces of hair you add to your own eyelashes. A reporter once asked my husband, "How do you stand all of her makeup?" He said, "What makeup?" I thought, That's how God sees it. He *doesn't*. He just sees me. He looks beyond the outside and sees the person inside.

In the big scope of things, what is a face, and of what value is it anyway? It just tells you that there's a person inside. That's all it tells you. When are we going to be able to look beyond a face? When are we going to be able to see the real person under the face? Why is a face so distracting to us?

Why do we judge people by their faces? *How* can we judge

people by their faces? Because they wear makeup, then they're vain? Because they don't, they're humble? Maybe it's the other way around. Without makeup, a person may feel ugly, and makeup makes them feel better about how they look. The person who doesn't think she needs makeup may be the vain one. She may think she's beautiful without it. Now, where is the vanity? The one who feels she needs improvement or the one who feels she doesn't need any improvement? See how foolish it all is?

My face is simply skin covering my bones. What I do with it should be my business, right? Ah, but here come the makeup police! The face patrol! They want to tell me what I can and can't put on *my* face. They decide not just about me, but about what all women should or should not put on their own personal faces. Now, to me that doesn't seem right.

Why do the cosmetic companies make all those tubes and bottles and boxes filled with beautiful colors if we're not supposed to use them? Why are some colors off-limits to some people? How can beautiful colors go out of fashion? Who makes these decisions? And when they're out of fashion, why do the cosmetic companies keep making these forbidden colors? Some women can wear blue and the fashion police don't bother them. But let me put even a hint of blue around my blue eyes and I hear the sirens screaming! Here they come! She's wearing *blue!* Get out the fashion police handcuffs.

Why is it that people they call models can get away with wearing all the colors at once? Now, let's see . . . what does that word "model" mean? I looked it up in Webster's just to make sure I clearly understood. Here it is: "A person or thing regarded as a standard of excellence to be imitated." That's what I thought it meant.

Now, there are many models. Do I get to choose which model I want to imitate? Can anyone be a model? Maybe I can be a model. Who's to say? The modeling agency? Why do we let them set the standard for what looks good and what doesn't? What looks good on me may not look good to somebody else—obviously, judging from all the flak I get on a daily basis. But why isn't my opinion as valuable as your opinion? See how silly it all sounds?

> Who made the rule that you don't put mascara on false eyelashes anyway?

Then there are those little pieces of hair that come in a little blue or pink box that everyone gets so upset about. I'm not even going to go there. Too many already have! I think those little pieces of hair might be the reason I'm getting to write this book! In people's minds they have gone from about a quarter of an inch to about a foot long. Wonder how they do that? It must be all that black mascara I put on them. Little fake hairs with black mascara on them—how can they cause such a stir? Must be a lot of bored people around . . .

I called this chapter "Tammy's Makeup Tips," so I guess for those of you who care, I'd better get to them.

First of all, I think every old barn can use a coat of paint. That quote is direct from good old C. M. Ward, who taught me in Bible college.

Second, I think only teenagers have enough natural beauty to get by without a little help from their friends. I have a girl-friend who's on TV every day. She wears more makeup than I have ever worn in my life. She is a really pretty woman and could probably do with a little less. However, I have seen her with no makeup on, and her face just disappeared. And she looked fifteen years older!

My face used to disappear without makeup, and I decided I don't do disappearing acts. (Bet you wish about now that I did!) So I went to a beauty parlor and had my eyes permanently lined, my eyebrows tattooed on, and my lips lined. Talk about pain. Now when I wake up in the morning it's all still there.

Believe it or not, I could just wear a little lipstick and look very put-together. But I can't help myself, I just have to add a little bit more. This is my morning routine and the products I use:

I get up and wash my face thoroughly with plain old Dial soap and water. In fact, I do that twice. After I have brushed my teeth with a tooth whitener, I put on my foundation. It's by Estée Lauder. It's called Double Wear; the color is Softan. I know it's a little darker than my skin, but it also serves as my tan. I never, *never* let the sun get on my face. As a result, my face is relatively unlined, even at my age. I have very good skin. I have not had a facelift as of this writing.

After I apply my foundation I do my eyes. I use L'Oréal Soft Effects eye color in Earthen Soft Perle on my brow bone. I put it on with my fingertips and rub what's left on my chin (it adds definition). I then take a little Almay Beyond Powder, Mother of Pearl, and use my fingertips to dab it on my eyelids. Brightens the eyes. Sometimes I will dab a little lavender on the inner corners of my eye, but not always.

Then I apply my lipliner and lipstick. I use any brand, any color. It's all about the same. Now, the fashion police say that the liner and lipstick should exactly match. I do it both ways, according to my moods. Sometimes I just feel like using darker liner and making the inside of the lip lighter. I often add shine, any kind.

I then add a little blush. I use any color you can buy at the drugstore but prefer the lightest blush I can find. I usually lean toward the light rose colors. I like warm colors. I use the blush on my cheekbones, my chin, and on my forehead. It gives the overall look of a healthy glow.

That's it! I'm done! It can take me five minutes or twenty minutes, depending on how long I want to play around with it.

Oops! Forgot the mascara. Obviously I put it on when I do my eyes. Oh, and I also take a little sponge applicator and put a little Earthen Soft Perle under my bottom eyelashes.

About my eyes . . . for me, adding darkness around my eyes makes them look bigger and more pronounced. The makeup people say that can't be so, but I have proven them wrong in my case. The secret to seeing what looks the best on you is to make up just one eye. Then you'll be able to see clearly which eye makeup does the most for *you*.

And gals, don't forget your feet! Polish those toenails! I don't care what age you are, pretty feet make you feel better about yourself.

The Makeup Store

I wish just once I could look in a mirror
And feel confident enough to walk out of here.
No eyes that are lined, no lashes long,
Just ME as I am, my heart filled with song.

I wish just once in the mirror I could see
A pretty face looking back at me,
Devoid of products man has made,
Content with only what God gave.

I feel good around my dogs; they don't care,
It's not what I look like, it's that I am there.
They don't judge me, they don't make fun,
They never hurt my feelings or make me want to run
Away where it doesn't matter anymore,
If I do or don't go to the makeup store.

Lessons
Worth
Learning

36.

Positive
or Negative

I have always been a positive person, or so I thought. So I was surprised when one day my daughter came up to me and said, "Mom, why are you always complaining?"

I was stunned! "What do you mean, Tammy Sue?" I asked.

She said, "Well, Mom, you're always tired or something is hurting."

I could not believe that she was talking about *me*. I decided that I was going to actually listen to what I was saying, that I was going to think before I spoke, that I was going to make myself aware. And what I heard when I became aware changed my life.

What did I hear myself saying?

"Oh, I'm so tired!" "Oh, my back aches, my knees hurt, I hate my hair, my head aches, I don't feel good."

I didn't say it all in one sentence, but I said it throughout the day, without even realizing it. Negativity had become a habit, complaining had become a habit, until I didn't even know I was saying those things.

I hear people every day speaking just like I did. I hear them sigh, I hear them complain about everything from the weather—it's too cold, too hot, it rains too much, it hasn't rained enough—to their kids, or their work; they're too fat, too tired, everything aches, on and on and on. They have developed a habit of complaining, and they probably don't even know they're doing it. It becomes a way of life and a source of conversation. Every conversation!

> YES and NO are the two most important words you will ever say. They determine your destiny in life.

I have never liked to be around people who are negative. It pulls me down and it's depressing. It's like being under a cloud on a sunny day.

Stop and think about people you love being around. What is it about them that draws you to them? Is it because they make you laugh? Is it because you feel better about everything when that person is around?

When Jamie was a teenager he was drawn to a group of kids I knew were going to change his life. And I was right. They drank and took drugs, and before long he was trying it too. I asked Jamie why he was drawn to that particular group of kids, when there were lots of kids around who didn't smoke, drink, and take drugs. What he said made sense to me. "Mom, they make me laugh!"

I have a friend I dearly love, but he has probably hurt my feelings more than any person I have ever met. He doesn't even realize he's doing it. He just talks, talks, talks, and forgets to listen to himself and what he's actually saying. He just says everything and anything that comes into his mind; he doesn't stop and censor things. We don't need to speak everything that is on our minds. Sometimes the best words are the ones left unsaid.

So I'm tired. Who cares? So my knee hurts—who cares? So I don't feel good on a given day—who cares? I often laugh to myself when someone automatically says as a greeting, "Hi Tammy, how are you today?" They don't really want to know the truth. They want to hear, "Oh, I'm just fine! Everything is great!" They smile and go on about their business. I often wonder what they would say if I said, "Oh, I feel awful, things are not going well at all." They would run in the other direction to avoid me the next time our paths crossed.

There is a verse in the Bible that says it so much better than I could ever say it: "Ye shall have whatsoever ye speak." Your words become a creative power. The children of Israel turned an eleven-day trip through the wilderness into a forty-year disaster because they murmured and complained. They spoke their fate into existence. Most of them died in that forty-year period and never got to see the promised land. All because of

> A bad habit never goes away by itself. It's always an undo-it-yourself project.
> —ABIGAIL VAN BUREN

their mouths, murmuring and complaining! If they would have kept their mouths shut and trusted in God who was taking such good care of them, it would have been a victorious eleven-day trip. Are we guilty of extending our troubles, of making things worse, because we can't stop our mouths from murmuring and complaining?

Can we turn the negative into positive by simply controlling our tongues? The Bible says that we can. Can we destroy our future, our promised land, by complaining about today? I believe we can. What can we do? We must make a conscious decision to listen to what we're saying. We must make a conscious decision to censor our speech. We must decide to engage our brains before we shoot off our mouths. We must make a decision to speak positive words every day, not negative words.

I have posted that scripture verse on my refrigerator—"Ye shall have whatsoever ye speak." It is a reminder for me every day. You must form a new habit. Breaking an old habit takes a while, but it is *not* impossible to do. Don't give up, keep working at being positive, and I guarantee you it will change your life too.

37.

Procrastination

My mother taught me many valuable lessons in life. One of those was *not to procrastinate*.

How did I learn this valuable lesson?

I was the chief dishwasher in our house, and the chief ironing person as well. Now, washing dishes back in those days was a major chore. You didn't just rinse them off and put them in the dishwasher. First of all, you had to heat the water—our faucet only ran cold water. Cold water and grease do not mix! After the water has been heated, you pour it all in the sink and put in your dishwashing soap (I liked Joy). You always wash the glasses first. Now, with ten people eating, you can imagine what came after the glasses: ten plates, ten sets of silverware, plus all the dishes that contained the food for ten people.

Then came the worst of all: the pots and pans. Yuck! Those greasy pots and pans! At that point you had to drain out the water, heat new water, and basically start over again.

My sister was supposed to be drying as I washed, but she had a way of disappearing. So nine times out of ten I ended up doing the whole task by myself.

I *hated* washing dishes. I'd try to talk my mom into allowing me to go out and play with the rest of the kids, and I'd promise to do the dishes later. She allowed me to do that one day, and I thought I'd really won the battle—only to find out that after two hours of sitting on the table the food had dried, the grease in the pots and pans was more disgusting than ever, and . . . well, it wasn't a pretty sight.

Then my mom sat me down and said, "Tammy, if you would have just got up and got the dishes washed, you could have played without worrying about having to come back in and do them later. And besides, you would not have had to scrape hardened food off the plates."

I learned the word "procrastination" that day.

If you have a chore to do, just get it done *now*. Don't put it off until later. I'll admit, I would fool around while doing the dishes after that. I'd throw soap at my sister, and she would hide a couple of the dirty pots and pans in the oven, only to reveal her joke after the last water had been let out of the sink. We'd fuss and fume—but the dishes always ended up washed, dried, and put away before I would go out and play with the other kids.

The same went with the baskets of ironing. I'd stand for hours and iron. But I didn't mind that nearly as much as I did the dishes. To this day, I *still* hate dishes! But I still do not procrastinate. I can't stand a messy kitchen. Thanks, Mom! And daily—well, almost daily—I thank God for wash-and-wear clothes.

Procrastination can throw your whole life off-kilter. It can make you a nervous wreck. Always putting off the inevitable can become a destructive habit. If you know it needs to be done, *just do it*. Get it over with!

I know people who always have a dirty house, are always late, their kids are always late, they're always in a hurry, yelling and screaming at each other. Why? They have always been procrastinators!

I had a girlfriend who died of breast cancer simply because she refused to make an appointment with her doctor. Her excuse was always, "Oh Tam, I promise I'll do it tomorrow." One day tomorrow never came for her. By the time she finally got around to actually making the appointment, it was just too late.

Kids fail in school because of procrastination. Businesses fail as a result of procrastination. Marriages fail as a result of procrastination. People die and go to Hell because of procrastination. They think, I'll get right with God tomorrow. But tomorrow never comes. Tomorrow turns into today, and then there's another tomorrow. With procrastinators there's always another time, or plenty of time— but time runs out, things pile up on them, they're always behind schedule . . . a life out of sync.

Stop procrastinating. You *can* change. It may take a change of attitude, but you can do it.

Start today. Make the bed as soon as you jump out of it.

Are you a woulda-coulda-shoulda person? Live for today! Yesterday is gone. It's like an egg that has been broken and can never be put back together again. Tomorrow may never come. So don't worry about tomorrow. Give today everything you have!

Hang up your clothes the minute you take them off. Then you won't have to iron them after they've been lying on the floor and walked on. Put those dishes in the dishwasher the minute you get up from the table. Then you don't have to sit and look at them.

We have a two-story house. When I see something lying around that needs to go upstairs, I take it as I go. That way stuff doesn't pile up. And then you don't have to make a lot of trips up and down the stairs loaded with things that could have gone up a little at a time.

Teach your children. They'll thank you someday. I will always be grateful to my mom for not allowing me to procrastinate.

Don't put off till tomorrow what you can do today. How many of us say, "Oh, one day I'll go see Mom and Dad. Oh, one day I'll get that fixed. Oh, one day I'll spend more time with my kids. Oh, one day I'll . . ." You fill in the blank. But the days go by so quickly. We're too busy with whatever it is we're doing, and we end up paying the consequences. We end up with regrets. Some people never become the people they were meant to be because of procrastination.

My friend, it's your choice! Make every day count! Especially today!

Do a job before it becomes overwhelming. Cut the grass while you can still get the lawn mower through it. Losing two or three pounds is easier than losing ten or fifteen pounds. I weigh myself every day, and if I've gained a pound or two, I work it off while it's still just a pound or two. I cut back on my eating and walk a few more minutes than I normally would.

If you see your children making mistakes, stop them while they're still *little* mistakes. When a snowball rolls downhill, it gathers speed and volume until it becomes almost impossible to stop.

There's an old saying: "I can take it in small doses." It's much easier to handle things in small doses. Don't wait until you have a situation that's impossible to swallow.

38.

Happy Miracles

The only big money I have ever spent on clothes is on Saint John Knits. I call them "forever clothes." No matter how many years it is in between adding a piece to your Saint John Knits wardrobe, the dye lots are always the same, so pieces always match. I am always looking for them in the resale shops, and once in a while I can find a piece that I like.

Last Christmas Roe and I were in New York, and he said, "Let's go to Bergdorf's or Saks Fifth Avenue. It's time that you have another Saint John Knit." I could not believe what I was hearing. I had not had a new one since PTL days. What I had was well worn.

I was so excited as we walked into Saks. I didn't have to just look at them this time and walk away wishing—I was actually going to get to buy one. My heart was pounding. I am a clotheshorse at heart. I literally ran to the Saint John Knits department, and before Roe even sat down, I zeroed in on the rack I wanted to look at. Black, of course. I'm so practical. I picked out a black jacket, like the one I've had since PTL days, which was looking a little worn. The saleslady came up as I was modeling it for Roe and said, "Tammy, how do you like this one?" It was basically the same jacket, but in the new three-quarter-length style. I tried it on, too, and wanted to have them both, but I could only have one. So after much debating back and forth with Roe, we decided on the regular jacket-length one. The sleeves needed to be shortened, so Roe insisted that I leave it there so they could send it to have the sleeves done at Saint John. I have never wanted to take anything home with me so bad in my life—unlike Roe, I am not a patient soul. Ha! But I knew I'd be so happy not to have to fold the sleeves under that I said okay. I was so happy as I walked out of that store, thanking my husband and thanking God. Still, I could not get my mind off the other jacket. But it was $990, and there just was no way.

Now it's nearly two years later and our ninth anniversary is coming up. This time we're in California doing *Hollywood Squares*. I wanted to spend a couple of days with my girlfriend, who's like a sister to me. So her husband and Roe went golfing, while Debra Lilly and I went shopping. We decided to go to the outlet mall, as we're both bargain hunters. She doesn't have to be, she just wants to, God bless Deb's heart!

When she told me the stores at the mall, she mentioned the Saint John Knits outlet first. I screamed, "Hey, Deb, I don't want to spend everything I have at one place." But we're girlies and weren't afraid to put ourselves in temptation's way. Again, my heart was racing as we neared that store. I jumped out of her Jag before it even stopped and was in the door before she had a chance to park. I always laugh and say I have a little shopping demon, and it's best not to cast it out lest worse come in its place. I also say that shopping is cheaper than a psychiatrist.

The store was fun but disappointing; they had nothing that I was interested in. No black! We were getting ready to walk out when the manager of the store said, "Didn't you girls find anything you liked?"

"No. I was looking for a three-quarter-length black coat, and you don't even have anything black. But thank you anyway."

She very calmly said to me, "Wait a minute, Tammy. I have one on hold in the back room. It's been there over a week and the lady has never contacted me about picking it up."

I said, "Well, please don't bring it out if it's on hold. If I see it I'll want it, and it belongs to her."

She said, "If you like it you can have it."

God answers kneemail!

I was so excited I thought I'd burst. She walked out from the back room with the exact coat I had wanted so badly two years earlier—and guess what? It was size eight, my exact size. And instead of $990, it was $490. I didn't have that much money with me, but isn't that what charge cards are for? I charged that coat before she could change her mind and was outta there!

I told Roe I had picked out my anniversary gift and he laughed. He was relieved he didn't have to do it.

I wore the new three-quarter-length jacket with my old Saint John Knits pants the night of our anniversary when we went to a beautiful restaurant for dinner. Inside my heart I was saying, "Thank you, Jesus, thank you, Jesus, thank you, Jesus!" On the outside I said, "Thank you, honey! I love it!"

I had been contacted by a company in California about doing a cartoon series. My think on it was, sure, everyone thinks I'm a cartoon character anyway, so I might as well really be one. I spoke with a man named Michael Faulkner. They began to write the scripts and design the characters. The first drawings of me they sent me I rejected. No! No! No! Tammy Faye wouldn't dress like that! She'd have on big rings, big bracelets, and her hair would be different. They ran with the changes and finally had me looking like Tammy Faye.

> Don't give up! Moses was a basket case!

Then they sent me copies of the first scripts. NO! NO! NO! Tammy Faye wouldn't say that, she'd never do that! She's a Christian! Well, we finally got the script worked out. I signed a contract saying that it had to be clean enough for my grandchildren and other kids to watch. They agreed. So many cartoons are so filthy, and I would not be a part of that.

Nearly a year passed. I would hear once in a while from Michael Faulkner that they were busy trying to sell it, but so far they hadn't. So I thought it was not going to happen, that it was just another dream.

My manager, Joe Spotts, Roe, and I were in New York. We decided to go shopping. Joe rented a car and let me go wherever I wanted to. I thought I'd died and gone to shopping heaven. At lunchtime, Joe said, "Let's try something we've never tried before," and we ducked into a tiny, tiny hole-in-the-wall Chinese restaurant. We thought it would be great, because only Asians were in there eating. Our lunch came. People were coming and going, but we paid no attention. The food was delicious and authentic, and we were enjoying the experience when I felt a tap on my shoulder. A man introduced himself and said, "Tammy, I am the president and CEO of the cartoon series you and Michael Faulkner are working on. I'm here in New York on business and just happened to see you when I walked in. I want you to know that we're still working on selling the project, and we are determined to get it done."

I could not believe what I was hearing. I had just met the headman! And he had actually talked to me. The cartoon *could* happen! I was excited and dumbfounded at the same time. What had just happened was not possible. That is, in man's eyes it was not possible. In God's eyes, *all* things are possible.

A few more months went by and I didn't hear anything, so once again I thought it just wasn't going to happen, when suddenly I received a call from Michael.

"Tammy, are you still interested in doing the cartoon? We have a huge TV network that picked out your cartoon from all the other projects I pitched to them. This is a big one, and I just wanted to know if you're still onboard. And guess what," he added, "they want it to be more religious! They said they thought you would have a unique perspective on religion."

Well, I wanted to cry. God had not forgotten. His timing is not our timing, and His timing is always right. If the other network they were pitching the cartoon to would have accepted it, I probably would have had a constant fight on my hands to keep it clean. Now here's a larger network that wants it to be even *more* Christian-oriented. God knows my heart, and He knows my desire to touch the hearts of young people. The cartoon is called *We Are Blessed,* and it's being produced by the people who produce *Rug Rats.* Maybe by the time you read this it will be on the air.

I can't wait to see what God is going to do next!

39.

A Fish Story— The One That Got Away

I have always loved animals of any kind. And I especially love fish. I could sit and watch them swim for hours. They have more personality than you would think. But I have not had much luck with keeping them alive for any length of time, even though I keep their bowl clean and make sure they're well fed.

A few years ago, I realized that I had not had fish for a long time, so I decided to get me a couple of goldfish. Tammy Sue, said, "Well, Mom, that's fine, but just don't name them and maybe you won't become too attached to them."

I thought that was a great idea. If they don't have names,

when they die maybe, just maybe, it will be easier for me to flush them down the commode.

Well, I don't know what I did differently, but after two years those two goldfish were still alive—and still unnamed. I began to feel guilty for not giving them names, so privately I called one Frick and the other Frack. Of course, you couldn't tell them apart, so if one did die, how would I know who it was?

Now, I've been having trouble with my eyes lately. My contacts have been giving me a fit. The other day I was sitting on the couch when I realized there was just one goldfish in the bowl. I looked again and then I looked again. Where could the other one have gone? It wasn't possible. I saw some water had splashed on the coffee table I kept them on, but I didn't think much about it; one of them was a jumper and often splashed water out of the bowl.

> Be good to your pets. Remember, they love you unconditionally. Give them a special treat today. Unlike people, they will never let you down.

And then I spotted him, lying on the carpet, deader than a doornail! He had jumped one too many times, and jumped right out of the bowl. Did he get claustrophobic and commit suicide? Or was he simply jumping for joy? He didn't leave a note, so I guess I'll never know.

I picked his little body up from the carpet and took it to the commode, but when I dropped him in, his little mouth started to move and his gills also started to move. I thought, Wow, a miracle! So I grabbed him out of the toilet, ran to his bowl, held on to his tail, and shook him back and forth. I guess that's what you'd call "artifishial" respiration, fish-style. His mouth was moving, and so were his gills, so I let him go. He immediately sank to the bottom like a rock. As he lay there, every sign of life went back out of him. Well, I didn't want to upset the other fish too much, so I reached down into the bowl, grabbed the dead fish by the tail, took him to the commode and, with a sigh of sadness, flushed.

I don't know if I flushed Frick or Frack, but whichever one is still swimming around seems really happy for the extra space. Who knows, he might have given the other one a little push.

I don't like to see anyone being alone, so I plan on getting another goldfish. They cost twenty-five cents apiece; that's a lot of joy for a small investment.

I might even take a chance and name the new one. I'm not sure. . . . I get attached awfully fast. And not knowing if it's a boy or a girl—well, we'll just have to think about it. My two little dogs are boys, so I just assumed the fish were boys too. I sure hope Frick or Frack, whoever it is that's left, will enjoy a new friend. He doesn't seem to be grieving over the old one!

40.

Famous People

Being in television as many years as I have, and working both in the Christian end of it and the secular end, I'm often asked, "Who have you met and what are they really like?" The thought always comes to my mind, Do you *really* want to know?

You may say, "Tammy, you sound a bit cynical." And I am. I admit it. I sometimes wish I had not even met some people I admired so much. People I thought would be so wonderful, like the characters they play on TV or in the movies. The key word here is *play*. As in imitate, portray, pretend to be . . .

Some famous people I have always wanted to meet include Marilyn Monroe, Katharine Hepburn, John Wayne, Lucille Ball, Elvis Presley, Audrey Hepburn, Doris Day, Rock Hudson, Dolly Parton, Elizabeth Taylor, Joan Rivers, and Sophia Loren. I know these people are all wonderful, that they're just like the people they imitate or portray in the movies or on TV. How do I know this? Because I haven't met them yet, or they died before I had the chance. So in my eyes they're everything I want them to be. They are kind, down to earth, fun, beautiful, perfect people.

Isn't it sad that some people are not like that? Believe me, I know. I've had my feelings hurt by the best—but also been surprised by the better!

Even as a little girl, I decided that I would be a *nice* famous person. Now, I couldn't imagine ever thinking in my wildest dreams that I, Tammy Faye LaValley, ever had any chance of actually being famous, or known anywhere but in the town of International Falls, where I was born and raised. I was so shy, I don't even know how my aunt Gin found out that I had a very clear, loud, contralto singing voice. I heard my grandma Fairchild say one time as I was sitting in front of the radio keeping time to the music that I had a good sense of timing and rhythm. I remember feeling so proud that I at least had some talent. After that I made a point of keeping time, counting out the beats of every song I heard. Was it three-quarter time or four-quarter? I have always loved music, so I figure I must have sung around the house. But before I knew it, Aunt Gin had me singing in church. I remember that making me very nervous. Then I began to sing at weddings and funerals. But I never felt that my singing was anything special. I think it was just that I was so little and so loud and so on key. And they tell me I was cute. Funny, I never felt cute. They tell me I was funny. Maybe I was making up for not feeling cute.

I have always had a funny bone. One thing I can remember about myself when I was young was that no matter who I was with, we were always laughing. My mom laughed a lot with us eight kids. I remember always teasing her and calling her "Rach." Her name was Rachel Minnie Fairchild LaValley

Grover. My mom also sang and played the piano and guitar. She had a fantastic voice. She was never allowed to sing or play the piano in our church because she was divorced. I thought that was mean. They would go without someone to play the piano rather than allow my talented mom to play. She was so hurt by that, as she had the calling of God on her life. She felt she had been called to the mission field, but before she could get there she married my daddy, who was a Catholic, and the Assemblies of God church disowned her.

Personally, I like the Catholic church. To me, people who attend the Catholic church go there to honor God. That's more than I can say for some churches I've been in.

As a child, I read a lot. I loved to read. Reading took me away from International Falls to wonderful places. I was always the romantic girl lead in every story. I had a way of actually living in a book. I would read at night with a flashlight under the covers in my bed. I still love to read and still have the ability to get lost in a good book. And I'm still the leading lady. I guess some of us never grow up.

I always have been a people pleaser. In my baby book Mom writes, *She will do funny things until you laugh. I think she needs a spanking!* So I guess I was born trying to please everyone and making people laugh.

I was also born with an extremely sensitive heart that could be broken very easily. I'd rather someone hit me than yell something mean to me. You can get over a slap, but it's hard to forget a mean remark yelled at you in anger. I'm still that way today. My husband is very hard of hearing. He is a gentle man who never raises his voice. I have a tendency to speak loudly to him most of the time, because he can't hear if the TV is on or people are talking around him. I was up in his office one day and was talking to him loudly just out of habit. He raised his voice at me and said, "You don't need to scream, I'm right here." It broke my heart right on the spot. It must have showed in my eyes; he immediately said he was sorry and put his arms around me as tears streamed down my face. I told him I thought we needed to learn some form of sign language. Laughter was not far behind.

I don't remember ever meeting any famous people as I was growing up. On radio you just pictured them in your mind. But, I have actually met many amazing ladies since those days. And leading men too. And I have learned that the people that I read about and fantasized about were much nicer than a lot of those I've actually met. I always give everyone the benefit of the doubt and assume that everyone is a nice person. That's where I've gone wrong. I guess I really have been very naive. They say that you think that people think like you do. You think that if you wouldn't do something, neither would they. You think that if you're capable of loving people and treating them with respect, then everyone else is capable of that too.

> Don't let the littleness in others bring out the littleness in you.

Well, I woke up to the facts of life when Jim and I were forced to leave PTL. I guess I grew up a lot! Reality is sometimes very hard to face. The Bible says we were born into this world sinners, full of unrighteousness. And it is only through God's saving grace that we can be good with His help. We're only good through Christ Jesus. And then in spite of everything we fail and need forgiveness.

I *have* met some wonderful famous people. People who don't

care who you are, they just love people. And they don't forget where they came from, and that there was a time when they were not famous. And they don't forget the reason they're famous: the people.

Unfortunately, then there are the ones that something happened to when they became famous. They don't realize how much they can hurt the people who love and look up to them. Or maybe they do and just don't care. Maybe being unkind is a kind of power.

Here's something I shall never forget. Jim was in prison in Rochester. Whenever I could afford to make the flight from Orlando to Minnesota to visit him, I would take my son, Jamie, to visit his daddy. Rochester is a sleepy little town, and after dark there's nothing much for a teenager to do. We were staying at the Kahler Hotel, and it was freezing cold outside. Jamie was bored, so he asked me if he could walk across the street to a mall that had a movie theater. I told him yes and away he went. A few minutes later he came back to the room looking so sad I could hardly stand it. When I finally got him to speak, he told me that a very famous country singer had rented the entire theater for the evening. He was standing in front of the entrance waiting for his people to show up, so Jamie Charles walked up to him and asked him if he could please have his autograph. The man refused, saying that if he gave Jamie an autograph he'd have to give everyone one. There was no one else around anywhere! My heart ached for Jamie. Jamie Charles was so excited to see this famous singer. He said, "Mom, I had a paper and pencil ready." I'm sure that man had no idea that here was a teenage boy who was hurting so badly. His dad was in prison, his whole life as he knew it had been taken from him, and an autograph, maybe ten seconds of the man's time, would have meant so much to him.

I hope I have never hurt anyone like that. If so, I truly apologize.

I'm glad I met the nice ones, I'm sorry I met the cruel ones, and I'm glad there are those I love whom I will never meet. That way I will never be disappointed. I can dream that John Wayne is the great hero, that Lucy is always fun and funny. I like it better that way. I want to meet Dolly Parton and Sidney Poitier, Elizabeth Taylor, Doris Day, Joan Rivers, Sophia Loren . . . or do I? Maybe I had better do what Grandma Fairchild said: "Tammy Faye, learn to leave well enough alone." Okay, Grandma.

No, I think I'll continue to take a chance. I *know* these are wonderful people!

P.S. In the past few weeks since I started writing this chapter, I've met Debbie Reynolds, M. C. Hammer, Snoop Doggy Dogg, and Melissa Rivers, Joan's daughter. I wasn't disappointed. I'm so glad!

41.

Use It
or Lose It

I have a friend who saves everything. She bought a
beautiful Brighton purse for which she paid over $200. I have
yet to see her use it, and that was months ago. The other day I
asked her why she wasn't using her beautiful leather purse. She
said she was saving it—she didn't want to wear it out or get it
scratched.

Now, this is an almost indestructible purse. It would last for
years if she used it every day.

She does the same thing with new clothes. And her house is
perfect. It doesn't look like anyone lives there. I have never
seen a speck of dust, anything lying around, a towel out of
place. When I visit her house I get tired just looking at all the
perfection. I keep finding myself wishing that just once I could
walk in and something, just anything—maybe a dish lying on
the kitchen counter—would be out of place. Even her garage
is perfect! A large sheet covers a still perfectly decorated Christ-

mas tree. Her husband actually washes her car before they drive it out of the garage. They are wonderful people and dear friends, but there are times I'd like to scream, "Hey you guys, give it a rest! Relax! Enjoy!"

Then there's *my* house . . . There's Tuppins and Muffin, whose whole life is a contest to see who can wee-wee the most. They have a big, fenced-in backyard that would make a grand watering place, and while they do water every bush and tree, they manage to save just enough to mark their territory in the house as well. I guess I use more Clorox Clean-Up than any human being alive.

Our house looks lived in. If you come to my house unannounced, you just have to take the good with the bad. The den is Roe's room. It's done in leather couches, bookcases, and easy chairs, with a fireplace. The coffee table is a huge piece of glass atop a golf bag filled with clubs, a huge bucket of golf balls, and golf shoes. It's a wonderful table I got him for his birthday. His room comes complete with newspapers lying around where he dropped them, two or three pairs of his shoes around his easy chair, empty cups and glasses that I *know* I just put into the dishwasher . . .

My living room would be perfect—we never go in that room, and it's gated off so the puppies can't either. But it looks like a museum! Mementos from the past cover every square inch of the room, including the baby grand piano. When I dust that room, it takes about a half a day . . . so therefore it doesn't get dusted often. So that room is *almost* perfect. The same with the dining room.

But when we have company over, down go the gates and we use every square inch. And it gets cleaned up again when I have time. Ten minutes after the guests have left, my friends' house would look like no one had ever been there. How does she *do* that?

Then there are the bedrooms and bathrooms. My two grandsons have their own room at our house. And when they come and spend the weekend and have all their neighborhood friends join them, well, need I say more? Roe and I have a very romantic bedroom, complete with a canopy bed draped in lace. But it's also my office, with my desk and typewriter. (Yes, I said typewriter. No computer for me.)

> Don't disturb the dust, it protects the furniture.

I love a made-up bed. Our bed is loaded with pillows and dolls. And no, Roe doesn't seem to mind. But getting all that stuff back on the bed every day just isn't going to happen.

I used to be a total perfectionist. I would almost go crazy if everything wasn't completely perfect. I nearly killed myself trying to keep everything perfect. One day my husband looked at me in frustration and said, "Who in the world sees this house every day?" When I said, "Just us," it dawned on me. I could relax a little and quit fretting if I didn't get everything done every day. It lifted an unbelievable load off me. I didn't have to feel like a bad housewife. I could let the guilt go and enjoy our home. I put up a little sign that says, "Don't disturb the dust, it protects the furniture." And I took a deep breath!

Now, our bathroom, no matter how many times I reorganize, it always looks like a storm came blowing through it. That storm is *me*. Makeup, wigs, hair curlers, animal-print towels, baskets, bottles (pretty bottles), jewelry cases, and two cute little doggie beds. That does not count the tub, shower, and commode. A delightful mess.

As for my husband's office . . . if I were still a perfectionist, I could never even open the door to that room. Building plans everywhere, computer equipment (ugly at best)—call it organized clutter. But I'm so glad to have him working at home that I could care less that everything within me says, "Clean it all out and start over again!" He keeps promising me that someday the builder in him will come out and it will be the most beautiful room in the house, and I believe him. I've seen the beautiful churches he has built.

I love an elegant house, but I love a lived-in look too. I guess I like casual elegance. Or cozy elegance. I believe in using everything—good dishes, good silver, tablecloths—everything, every day. After all, who are we saving everything for? In all probability, our children have different taste than we do, so when we leave this world it will just be sold. So why shouldn't we enjoy the fruits of our labor while we can? Who cares if something gets broken or chipped? It's just *stuff*. Everything can be replaced, except the people we love.

42.

Drifting
Away

My grandsons, James (twelve) and Jonathan (eleven), love to swim. And above all, they love to swim in the ocean. Every year we take them to the ocean, which is just a few hours from our house. We spend three or four days in a hotel. We spend days on the beach, nights eating out and letting the kids go on the rides that go for blocks down the beachfront. We eat ice cream and cotton candy until we almost turn pink, go back to the hotel, sleep a few hours, and start over again the next day.

Our trips to the ocean are bittersweet for me. I love being with the boys and doing something so special with them, but by the time we arrive back home every nerve in my body is frayed. Let me explain.

The minute the boys hit the soft, warm sand of the beach they take off like lightning has struck them. They run to the water and away they go. Grandma's eyes try to spot them among the hundreds of other kids who are also on vacation. And I have tried everything I know to keep them in view. We always buy them brightly colored floats, the kind that can be fastened around the wrist. Then bright headbands to further help identify them among the other hundreds of kids. But after a while, no matter what you've done, they all look alike, and a panic begins to set in. Even though they are excellent swimmers, it's easy to wander out too far and get into trouble in unfamiliar waters.

One afternoon sitting on the beach I thought I'd take the opportunity to relax a little and read a book. When I looked up after reading for a few minutes, the boys were nowhere in sight. My heart began to pound; panic took over my entire body. I jumped to my feet and began running down the beach like a woman gone mad, screaming over the thunder of the waves, "James, Jonathan, James, Jonathan, where are you?" I felt like one little grain of sand on that large beach. There was no way they were going to see me, much less hear me in the midst of the huge crowd of people and the roar of the waves.

I ran and I ran and I ran, my breath coming in huge gulps. My legs were fighting against the sand that was holding me back and the waves that were lapping around my ankles. I could not see the brightly colored headbands. I could not find the boys.

By that time, terrible thoughts were running through my mind. They had swum out too far, a riptide had caught them and pulled them under. Maybe someone had kidnapped them. Where were James and Jonathan? I had promised their mom that I'd take good care of them. Those boys were my very heart. Love flooded over me for them. At the same time, I thought if I found them I was going to really give them you-know-what for not staying where they were supposed to stay, in front of our hotel. *Boys, make sure you stay in front of the hotel.* We had talked about it. They had promised. *Yes, Grandma, we'll swim in front of the hotel.*

I ran until my legs threatened to collapse. I didn't know what was going to go first, my legs or my lungs or my voice. I was frantic. About five hotels down I finally spotted two little headbands, bright orange and bright red. James and Jonathan! I screamed for them to come back. I screamed for them to come in. To no avail! They didn't even know they were lost. Finally someone saw my distress and swam out and told the boys I wanted to talk to them. They came out of the water, I'm sure wondering, *What in the world is wrong with her?* I began screaming—or should I say continued screaming. "Why are you guys so far down the beach? You promised Grandma that you would swim only in front of the hotel. I'm never bringing you to the beach again!"

Then they said something that shocked me. "Grandma, we thought we *were* in front of the hotel. We must have just drifted." They were actually shocked to find out how far they had gotten from the hotel, their landmark. It was then I realized that the ocean is such a powerful force that you can easily drift out too far, or over too far, and not even know it. The boys were just having fun and had no idea they had drifted so far away.

I apologized to them and let them get back in the water to swim back to the front of the hotel. But I never again relaxed while they were swimming.

I have since thought about that experience. Thought about how easy it is in life to drift away from our dreams for the future, to drift away from our convictions, to drift away from our friends and family, to drift away from God. James and Jonathan were just doing what kids do when they get in the ocean. They were just enjoying themselves, just having fun. They were not thinking about the dangers of the big ocean, or of getting lost in the midst of so many thousands of people. They were not thinking that their hotel wasn't in front of them anymore. They were focused on having fun and enjoying the experience of freedom the ocean gave them. They lost their landmark and didn't even know it.

The Bible says that King Solomon was the wisest and most intelligent man on earth at the time. He possessed all the worldly goods a man could possess. He had many, many wives, he had servants, he had wealth, and he was highly intellectual. Yet even Solomon, in all his glory, drifted away from God.

The Bible says that David was a man after God's own heart. Yet he saw a beautiful woman and his heart began to lust, and he drifted away from the close walk he'd had with God. He went so far as to have the woman's husband murdered so that he could have her as his wife.

Two of the greatest men in the Bible, both caught up in the ocean of life. Both lost their focus and drifted away.

We are all capable of drifting away from God, drifting away from our values in life; we are all capable of losing sight of our landmark. Some drift off into eternity without God, hopelessly lost. Others realize they can't see "the hotel" anymore, and they fight their way back through the waves and the current.

I often think of that Grandmother, that Mom, that Dad who won't give up until they see those heads bobbing in the ocean of life once again. They keep praying even though they are worn out, even though they are tempted to give up hope. They persist. Prayer changes things. Prayer makes the impossible possible. There is nothing too hard for the Lord. We must not give up. We must keep our eye on the goal.

43.

The Devil Has No Pitchfork or Tail; He Is Beautiful

Beauty can be dangerous! Very dangerous! The other day my girlfriend was visiting me for a few days. She had never been to North Carolina and was fascinated by a beautiful vine that grows up many of our trees. The vine can take over everything in a very short time. She asked me what it was, and I said "kudzu." She kept saying how beautiful it was.

Then I asked her if she realized the kind of trees it was clinging to. Dead trees! Trees that were thriving before the beautiful kudzu vine came along. What it does is choke the tree to death. It wraps around and around the tree, growing up to the very top. Eventually, it saps all the life from the tree and it dies.

Las Vegas is the most beautiful place I have ever seen. The beauty and excitement of that town make the heart beat faster. It never closes. Day turns into night and night turns into day, and if you're inside one of those beautiful buildings you never know it. It's a place where time stands still. But the beauty and excitement of that town have ruined so many lives forever. It has bankrupted people who had a wonderful future ahead of them, financially and emotionally and spiritually.

Drugs can be a beautiful experience, I am told. If they weren't, what would hold people in their power? People tell me about the extreme "high" they get when they take drugs, and consequently they become so dependent on them they will do anything it takes to continue taking drugs. People die of drug overdoses almost every day somewhere. But they're willing to take the chance because it is such a "beautiful" experience. It makes you feel good!

I have seen with my own eyes what drugs can do. Most of us have. I think almost everyone can tell a story of how drugs destroyed a career, a relationship, or someone's health. One day my son told me he had been taking drugs and had also started to drink and smoke. I asked him about the cigarettes first and he said, "Mom, the cigarette is my friend. With it in my hand I have courage."

I thought about that for a few minutes and then told him, "But honey, it's a friend that will end up killing you. What kind of friend is that?"

Drugs will give you a good time, then they turn on you and destroy your life. As will alcohol. One day Jamie realized this and gave his life entirely to God. God gave Jamie a miracle. He delivered him from drugs and alcohol and cigarettes, and now he is preaching the Gospel. He's a great preacher and is working with kids who are living the life he once lived. He's able to help them because he has walked in their shoes and knows what they face each day. He understands what drugs can do to the mind and the body—and most of all, to the soul.

44.

"There is a way that seemeth right unto man, but the end thereof is destruction"

This was my father's favorite Bible verse. He also loved the verse "Broad is the way and narrow is the path and few there be that find it."

I wish everyone could go to Heaven when they die. And I know that the heart of Jesus is love, and that is what He, too, wishes. In fact, He so wanted everyone to go to Heaven that He gave his life on the cross of Calvary so that everyone would have that opportunity. He didn't have to die for lost humanity: He *chose* to die for us. By His death He paid the ultimate sacrifice for our sins.

But there is a condition we have to meet to take advantage of his death for us. We have to choose to admit that we are sinners and ask Him to forgive us our sins. For all have sinned, the Bible says. Mother Teresa has sinned, Billy Graham has sinned, all of our spiritual leaders have sinned and have had to choose to ask for God's forgiveness of those sins.

You might say, Well, I am a good person. I give to all the right causes, I live a clean life, I help the poor, etc. The Bible says, it is not of works any man should boast. We cannot give our way into Heaven with money or good deeds or living a good life. The Bible says *you must be born again.* That means all of us! No one is exempt from this command.

I feel that all babies who die go directly to Heaven. Why? Because the Bible speaks of "the age of accountability." There is much debate over when a child reaches that age. Some feel that children are accountable for their deeds and have an understanding by age twelve. Some feel the age is younger than that. I know that at the age of ten I felt that I needed to accept the Lord as my personal Savior. I felt the need to repent, of what I wasn't sure, but I asked Jesus to forgive me of my sins and come into my heart. I will never forget that day, because I felt so different after I prayed that prayer. I knew that if I died that day, I would go to Heaven.

Sometimes I think it's easier as a child to accept God into

your life. Children don't ask a lot of questions. You read the Bible to them, their little hearts open up and they simply believe. Adults question and analyze and debate themselves right out of believing. I think it's just too easy for them. If they had to do penance, walk over glass, crawl on their knees for miles, or sacrifice something, they would feel they had done something to deserve forgiveness. But simply asking? They have a hard time with that. It can't be that easy! But it is that easy. John 3:16 says, "For God so loved the world that He gave His only begotten son, that whoever believes in him should not perish but have eternal life." Period.

> No matter how far down the wrong road you go, it can never become the right road.

God loves us all just the way we are, all full of sin. But He gave us a way out. He made it possible for us to change. He died to change our sinful nature into His nature. He wants us to become like Him.

When the Bible says God wants us to be born again, it means just that. The first time we are born, we emerge from our mother's womb. The second time we are born is through the shed blood of Jesus on Calvary. That rebirth takes a sinful nature, sinful thoughts, and sinful deeds and cleanses us from all unrighteousness.

God has given us a conscience. And I believe that we instinctively know when we are doing wrong. But our conscience can be scarred by continually ignoring that inner voice that says you're doing something wrong. The first time you tell a lie, you feel awful. The second time you tell a lie, it becomes a little easier, and each time we tell a lie that little voice inside us gets weaker and weaker and weaker until we can't hear it at all anymore and we have talked ourselves into thinking it's all right to lie. Even though the Bible plainly says it's a sin to lie and all liars will find their place in Hell.

So what do we do to restore that conscience? We go back and read what the Bible says about, in this case, lying, and we simply ask God to forgive us and help us not to do it anymore. We have to once again become conscious that we are doing wrong, according to God's word. I believe that is the only way to restore a conscience that has been destroyed. God's word is His word! It's what He wants from us. He means what He said in His word. And if we are going to live a life pleasing to Him, we must obey His word, the Bible.

There is no sin that cannot be forgiven except the sin of constantly turning your back on that little voice called the Holy Spirit, the one that says, "Ask for forgiveness." You know when you hear it. And you know the uncomfortable feeling you feel when you intentionally turn away from the God who created this universe.

There are so many questions that people ask when they do not want to make a commitment to God. They ask:

Why would a God of love send me to Hell?

Answer: Because He gave you a will to choose Him or not to choose Him, and He will not go against your will.

Why does God allow bad things to happen to good people?

Answer: I, too, have asked that question and have come to the conclusion that I don't know the answer. One thing I do know is that God loves everyone exactly the same. And why He allows some to be murdered, to die of sickness, to suffer untold agony I do not know, but I do know that if they have accepted Jesus as their personal Savior they will go to Heaven, where there is no more hurting, no more sickness, no more sadness—and no more questions!

Can God protect us?

Answer: *Yes*. He says, "He will give His angels charge over us to keep us in all our ways." So according to the Bible, we have a guardian angel. But the Bible also says, "It is appointed unto man once to die and after that the judgment." We do not know when that appointment is, nor how it will come about. That is one reason to talk to God every day, and if you sin to ask His forgiveness. I pray every night and ask God to forgive me. It's probably not necessary to do that, but I love to talk to God. It is just a part of who I am. Let Him be a part of who you are. It will bring you great peace of mind.

Do not let questions keep you from asking God to forgive you of your sins. There are some questions that there are no answers to. So why waste our time and energy asking why, why, why?

And remember, no matter how far down the wrong road you go, *it can never become the right road.* You need to stop, turn around, and start again. God is the God of second chances and third chances. He loves you and will forgive you of anything, if you will just admit you are wrong and ask Him to.

There are three letters in the word SIN. My friend Sarah Utterback came up with a saying that really says it simply:

SIN: Stop It Now

And that's all we have to do. Ask Jesus to forgive us our sins, and then stop sinning, turn around, and go the other direction.

45.

Planting Seeds

Have you ever planted a seed and waited excitedly for it to sprout and grow? I think every child has done that in school. I remember my kids bringing home a Dixie cup with a seed they had buried in the small bit of dirt the cup contained. They would water and watch. I would warn them with motherly love that a watched pot never boils, so they would finally quit checking on it every day. Then one day they would come running, carrying the little cup containing a brand-new sprout. "Hey Mom, it worked!"

Yes, it works! If you plant a seed it will eventually grow. Particularly if watered. If not, it will wither and die.

Everyone plants seeds, whether you are aware of it or not. Seeds of joy, seeds of peace, seeds of confidence, seeds of faith. We plant seeds of some kind into people's lives every day. Some of those seeds grow slowly, some of those seeds sprout almost immediately. And we can see them come to the top of those lives we plant them in. My daughter, Tammy Sue, tells me constantly of seeds of faith that her dad and I unknowingly planted in her life many years ago. Thankfully, they grew, became strong, and are still healthy in her spirit today. She has such great faith, in spite of the terrible circumstances she has had to suffer through.

You can plant seeds and not even know it. Nature shows us that. All kinds of animals plant seeds unknowingly through the digestive process. Even the wind has a part in seeding the world.

You carelessly tell a child in anger, "You're so stupid!" Or you say, "I wish you'd never been born!" Or, "You're fat!" We've all slipped and said things we wished we never had.

Children themselves plant seeds. They sometimes parrot the things they hear at home. Mom or Dad said it, so it must be true. Children can plant cruel seeds without even knowing what they say, without realizing that when they make fun of someone it could ruin a life forever. We see that in the school bombings. What did the perpetrators say? They just couldn't take the things the kids said to them anymore. I think we all remember at least something that was said to us in school that hurt us.

There are many great examples of seed-planting. Your co-worker walks into your office feeling great, looking great—she thinks. Then someone says, "You look a little pale, don't you feel well today?" I feel great, she replies, but a seed has just been planted in her fertile mind: "They say I look pale. Maybe I don't feel as well as I thought. I must *look* awful! I'm getting a headache and my stomach doesn't feel so good either. Maybe I'm coming down with something." Her day has been ruined because of a little seed planted by some unthinking co-worker.

Karen Carpenter read something about herself that planted a deadly seed in her mind. A reporter said she was fat. As a result, she became an anorexic and eventually died a premature death. A stupid reporter, a deadly seed! One of the greatest voices of our time, gone!

How many people have missed becoming all they could be because someone planted a seed in their mind? You're not good enough, you're not pretty or handsome enough, you're not smart enough, you're too shy, you don't have enough money to do that, you'll never be able to do *that!* Those seeds can grow and grow and sap the creativity right out of a person. Those seeds of doubt, placed there by people who don't have a clue what they're planting into lives.

> It is always better to fail in doing something than to excel in doing nothing.

I love being around children and young people. They're so full of life and creativity. They feel they can do *anything,* that they can be anything, and that they can have *everything.* My heart aches as I see their dreams destroyed one by one by those they come in contact with in life.

Are you a discourager or an encourager? Do the words of your mouth encourage or discourage those around you?

I loved my grandmother Fairchild. She was an encourager. I always felt like I could do anything after I left Grandma's house. The same with my aunt Gin.

"Now Tam, you can do this." I can still hear her.

"No I can't, Aunt Gin," I'd reply.

"Don't you tell me that, Tammy Faye. You can too!"

She didn't let me get away with saying I can't do it, it's too hard, or I'm not good enough.

I was so fortunate to have those strong, positive women around me. They planted seeds into my life that still grow strong and healthy today. They took a little, shy, backward, scared-of-her-own-shadow girl and planted seeds of confidence in her. "That kid can sing, she is so funny, she has great timing, she can do anything she sets her mind to." Those seeds were planted in my mind at a very young age. They did not know they were planting them. I did not know they were planting them. But as I began to want to do things in life, I realized these seeds had grown and given me confidence. I *could* do it, because Grandma and Aunt Gin said I could.

I have had so many seeds of doubt planted in my mind by the media, by people who don't like me. Seeds like, "She can't sing. She has no talent. Her makeup looks awful! She doesn't know how to dress. She'll never make it without Jim Bakker. She'll never do anything again."

The only thing that has stopped these seeds from taking root in my mind has been the power of God in my life. "I can do all things through Christ which strengthen me." I absolutely *re-fuse* to let these seeds germinate in my mind. The thought that maybe, just maybe, they're right flies over my head, but I don't let it land. Not even for a minute. Fly away, bird!

The Bible says, "Resist the devil and he will flee from you!" We need to resist those negative thoughts and replace them with positive thoughts like, I can *too* do it! If anyone in the world has ever done it, so can I! And if they haven't, I'll be the first!

If you can dream it, you can make it happen! Believe in yourself! No one else can do it for you! You must make it happen!

Never give up. Keep trying. Just keep plugging away. Roe is a contractor, and he says, "If you throw enough mud against the wall, some of it is bound to stick."

As a little girl I dreamed of being on the Grand Ole Opry.

It sure seemed like a pipe dream at the time, utterly impossible. But guess what—on my fortieth birthday I sang on the Grand Ole Opry!

Jim Bakker, a young kid from Muskegon, Michigan, had a dream of doing a Christian talk show like Johnny Carson's. He never gave up on that dream, even though there were so many discouraging times, and he ended up building the world's largest Christian TV satellite network and was the originator of the very first Christian talk show, *The 700 Club*. He never gave up! He persisted! People told him it wouldn't work, he couldn't make it happen, there was not enough money for his dream— but he never gave up. Plus, he taught hundreds of other people how to make it happen for themselves. He would not allow the seeds that people were trying to plant in his mind to settle long enough to germinate.

Jealous people plant seeds, angry people plant seeds, people who do not have faith plant seeds, judgmental people plant seeds, well-meaning friends plant seeds, family members plant seeds, clergy plant seeds, husbands and wives plant seeds in each other's lives, the media plant seeds. . . . *Be careful whose seeds you allow to take root in your mind!*

A final word to all of us, including myself: Be careful what you say! Get your mind in gear before you put your mouth in motion. Don't spout off all the time. Don't be that person who's "always right!" No one is always right. I don't want to be around people who think they're always right, because they aren't. We can all make mistakes of judgment.

Encourage the dreams of your children, your friends. The kindest words are the ones left unspoken. Don't just talk to be talking all the time. Think!

And when someone discourages you, pray and ask God to

help you. He cares about anything concerning you. Ask God to open doors you should walk through, and ask Him to close doors you should not walk through. I pray that prayer every day. Yes, I hear what people around me say, both discouraging and encouraging, but the buck stops only with God. I work toward making things happen, but if they don't, I thank God for closing that door. And I am not discouraged. I am praising the Lord. And I work toward the next dream.

"She's too old to do that . . ."

Wanna bet?

46.

Shopping Center Kids

I decided to go to the Palm Springs Mall to do some shopping. I was busy doing just that, when all of a sudden I heard my name being called very loudly. I tried to figure out where it was coming from and was becoming more embarrassed by the minute.

"Tammy Faye! Tammy Faye!"

Now everyone was looking up—and there on the second story of the mall were four teenage boys.

"You're rich, Tammy Faye, buy us something. Why don't you buy us something?"

It was becoming a taunt. I was trying to figure out what to do without further embarrassing myself. I decided to take the high road and have fun with the kids.

I yelled back up to them, "Hey, guys, come on down and I'll buy you lunch."

"Aw, you're kidding," they said.

"No, we'll eat at Marie Callender's here in the mall. Yes, I really mean it."

I have never seen such a drastic change as I saw in those teenage boys. They literally ran down the escalator, and within a couple of minutes all five of us were walking side by side.

"Are you really gonna take us to eat?"

"I sure am," I answered.

"Man, we gotta call our moms. Hey Joe, you got the cell phone?"

By that time we arrived at Marie Callender's and were immediately seated. Then the boys did something very unexpected. They tucked their shirts into their pants, they removed their baseball caps and smoothed their hair. One of them said, "Hey, man, we gotta look good if we're gonna eat with Tammy Faye Bakker! Hey, man, our moms will never believe this!"

> A smile is the shortest distance between two people. Give someone a smile today.

I told them they could get anything they wanted. They were dumbfounded! "Anything?" they cried.

"Yes, anything. Plus dessert if you want."

"Wow, damn, nobody is gonna believe this."

They did not take advantage of me, as they well could have. They ordered hamburgers and french fries. They finally got their moms on the cell phone, one by one. "Hey, Miss Faye, will you talk to my mom? She won't believe it's really you." Sure, I said, and proceeded to talk to Mom.

The boys and I sat there and talked teenage talk for over an hour. It was one of the most wonderful hours I've ever spent.

No telling how long it had been since an adult had listened to them talk. We ate and laughed and talked, then we ordered dessert.

As we went to leave, one of the boys piped up, and I will never forget what he said as long as I live:

"Miss Faye, one day I'm gonna be rich. When that happens I'm gonna come and pick you up in a big limousine and take you out to dinner."

I told him I would look forward to that. After hugs and lots of thank-yous, four totally different attitudes walked out of that restaurant. I had just made four new friends. It was the best $50 I have ever spent!

47.

The Gay Community

People often ask me when and why I got in-
volved with the gay community. Some ask it kindly, some with
disdain in their voices. I am constantly judged by the Christians for loving "the gays."

It all started twenty-something years ago, when I did a daily
show called *Tammy's House Party*. It was at a time when HIV-
AIDS had just been discovered, and it was largely at that time
a gay disease. People were in a panic and did not even want to
breathe the same air as a person who had AIDS. Those poor,
suffering people were treated as if they had leprosy. My heart
ached at the way they were being treated. Their families even
stayed away from them. Because of a disease, they were ostracized.

I felt that as Christians it was our responsibility to help these
suffering people. We were the ones who should be putting our
arms around these people, praying for them, encouraging them.

I felt that by interviewing a gay man I would open people's eyes to understanding, to compassion. Jesus would have been walking among them were He on earth. I so wanted to be His hand extended. We sing that song "Oh, to be His hand extended, reaching out to the oppressed, let me touch Him, let me touch Jesus, so that others may know and be blessed." Tears stream down our faces as we raise our arms to God, singing that song. Then we walk out of the church and forget it. I didn't want to forget it. I really meant it when I asked God to let me be His hand extended. Our hands are really the only hands He has. Our arms are the only arms Jesus has. I didn't have any idea what that simple act of interviewing a gay man would lead to. It ended up being a life-changing experience.

You might say, "But we were afraid." Fear is the opposite of faith. Fear activates the devil the way faith activates God. Sure, it is human to be afraid, but I refused to allow fear to stop me. And because of that, God has allowed me to do things most people will never get to do, to go places most people will never get to go. And God has protected me and taken care of me in every situation. I still get scared, but I still continue to step away from my fears and get on with life. And as a result, my light shines in the strangest places! I'm not afraid that sickness will jump on me, I'm not afraid that the devil will jump on me. My Bible says that He gives His angels protections over me; He says that "no harm shall come nigh me." He tells me that if I eat any deadly thing it shall not harm me.

I remember our whole team was doing a telethon in a little town. We were preaching and singing and working so hard. That night we all decided to go out to eat. There were about fifteen of us, and most of us ordered the patty melt hamburger with cheese on it. Jim and I were among the patty melt gang. Tammy Sue was about four at the time, and she wasn't hungry that night. I tried and tried to get her to eat some of my food, but she wouldn't.

Later that night everyone who had eaten the patty melt began to get terribly sick. The singers ended up in the hospital, fighting for their lives, and Jim and I were so sick we could not even turn over in bed. We spent two or three extra days at a motel, too sick from food poisoning even to get out of bed. We kept claiming God's word. And we all made it. I thank the Lord to this day that Tammy Sue refused to eat that night.

Then a great blessing came to us months later as a result of going through the food poisoning episode. It was Christmas, and we had no money to buy gifts for anyone. We went to the mailbox one day and to our amazement there was a check from the law firm of the restaurant chain. They had sent everyone involved a check. It stated that if we signed the check we could not file a lawsuit against the company.

We had the greatest Christmas we ever had that year. A miracle Christmas! And all because God had kept His word to us. If you eat any deadly thing it shall not hurt you. It made us horribly sick, but there were no permanent complications. And we received a blessing on top of it, and a testimony.

That's the reason I felt comfortable working with people with AIDS. I felt that God would protect me, and I still feel that way. I have probably hugged and kissed more people with AIDS than anyone. I have cried with them, laughed with them, eaten with them, and I have ministered to them. The gay community has enriched my life, and I hope I have made their lives a little bit better.

It was the gay community that took care of me when I was hurting so badly that I wanted to die. I just wanted the Lord to take me home to Heaven. My second husband had been sent to prison, I was all alone, I felt abandoned by everyone, even sometimes by God. The days were so long and the nights even longer. Loneliness enveloped me like a tight garment. It was always there, haunting me, tormenting me. Where were all the people who'd said they loved me? Where were all the thousands and thousands of people I had ministered to for so many years?

The media said I was famous. What exactly did that mean? If you were famous, you couldn't be lonely and alone. It was then that I coined the saying, "Fame is an elusive shadow." A shadow only shows up when you have light shined on you. In the darkness it hides. Fame is like that—you can see a shadow, but you can never get ahold of it; no matter how you chase your shadow you will never touch it, feel it, or catch it. It's just a shadow.

But then something wonderful happened in the midst of my hurt. The gay community! "Tammy, we love you!" And they proved it over and over and over again. One gay man sent me $10,000 tax-free! He knew I did not have medical insurance, and he said the money was for any emergencies I might have. He had watched me on PTL and had seen the show I did with a gay man.

More gay men began to enter my life. They helped pay my bills while Roe was in prison—and I never once told anyone but God that I needed help. They sent me checks every month. They sent me gifts on special occasions and for Christmas. They sent me beautiful things—clothes, jewelry, flowers. They overwhelmed me with the love I no longer felt from the Christian community.

Christians now tell me that they didn't know where I was—that they couldn't find me. And I'm sure that's true. But the gay community found me, and I will love them forever. They gave me so much more than gifts and money. They gave me unconditional love. They gave me their time. They wrote to me, they called me, they made me feel special. They still make me feel special. They still make me feel loved. And I hope in some small way I give back to them just a little of what they have given to me. I minister in gay churches, I now minister through email. I do many gay benefits, helping to raise money for AIDS patients and their families. I speak for them all over the country.

> The reason you find life an empty dream is because you put nothing into it.

Being a heterosexual, I do not even pretend to understand the gay lifestyle. I don't think that heterosexuals ever will understand. But that does not mean that we can't care for each other, that we can't love each other, that we can't help each other. So many of my close friends are gay. As my heterosexual friends do, they stay in our home when they're in town for a visit.

My gay friends still know my stand on homosexuality. We are able to discuss it openly. They know what the Bible says about homosexuality as well as I do. They can quote more scriptures on the subject that any of *you* can, I think. Most of the gays I meet say they were born that way. They're not flip about it.

They are dead serious. They discuss with me their fears, their hopes, their dreams. We talk about God, about Heaven and Hell. They allow me to ask questions. They allow me to disagree with them, because they know I'm not out to hurt them but am talking to them in love. God leads in peace!

Jim J Bullock, the man I did a TV show with for a year, is a gay man. He loves me and I love him. He says publicly, "I know Tammy doesn't agree with our lifestyle, but that doesn't affect our friendship."

Christians ask me if I am still a Christian. That breaks my heart! The Bible says to "go into all the world and preach the Gospel to all creatures." We are all God's creatures! He created us. He loves us. What they're intimating is that because I go where they won't go, I am no longer a Christian. To me that is a direct misinterpretation of God's word. I believe that this big old world contains millions of little worlds, and each person has their little world. If I came to your house, I would be entering your world. I would be a part of your family, your friends, I'd eat what you eat, I'd shop where you shop, I'd go to church where you go to church, I'd ride in your car or truck or on your motorcycle. I'd live in your world. I think that is what the Bible means when it says go into *all* the world. If you reach the one next to you, and I reach the one next to me, in no time at all we'll have them all. That's a little song we used to sing in Sunday school. It's about everyone reaching out to the one next to them.

I love Jesus more than life itself. He is my best friend. My desire is to serve Him with my life. And my desire is to tell others of the change He alone can make in a life if you will just allow Him to. He will bring peace where there is no peace, joy where there is no joy, comfort to a heart that is aching, healing to a body that is sick. He has done all of that for me. I would not be alive today if it were not for my faith in an almighty God. Salvation is available to all. We are all sinners, for all have sinned and come short of the glory of God. God does not categorize sin. We do that. To God, sin is sin. Lying is a sin. How many Christians lie all the time and think nothing of it? Yet the Bible clearly states that all liars will spend eternity in Hell.

Is that part not for us? Are we guilty of only believing the parts of the Bible we agree with? Or is it that we don't really know what our Bible says? Have we become so intelligent that we have changed the Bible to fit our thinking? I have always taken the Bible to say what it means and mean what it says. I have heard preachers interpret the Bible their way, I have seen people of different faiths interpret it their way, and people of different sexual persuasions interpret it their way. I have heard preachers preach "the deep things of God."

Yet I think the Bible remains a relatively simple book, containing a simple plan of salvation, teaching us how to live, giving us examples of people like us, going through trials like we do. It tells of Heaven and it tells of Hell, Heaven being prepared for those who accept Jesus as their personal Savior and live a life pleasing to Him; Hell, a place prepared for those who do not accept the plan of salvation, and a place prepared for Satan. You can choose to either believe it or not. God himself gives us that choice. You can alter what the Bible says, but that does not change it. You can say what you want about the people who wrote the scriptures. But God uses people, and the Bible says it is the inspired word of God. You can take chances that it's not true—that's your decision. As for me and my house, *we will serve the Lord!* I'm not going to take a chance with my eternal soul. I choose to serve the Lord. It's a great way to live. It has worked for me!

What's wrong with peace and joy and love and healing? What's wrong with believing that the angels of the Lord surround you, protecting you from harm? What's wrong with believing in a Heaven where there will be no more sickness, no more tears, no more heartaches, no more dying, and spending eternity with my best friend, Jesus?

48.

Jesus Is Coming

The other day I was watching a TV program on Christian television, something I rarely do these days. Two preachers were talking about the war in Iraq and the fact that we were watching the Bible "come to life" right in front of our eyes. Everything that is in the daily newspapers was actually written about hundreds of years ago . . . in the Bible!

When I was a child, I was taught that Jesus could return any day. I believed with all my heart that Jesus would come in my lifetime. I used to think that Jesus would come before I even had a chance to get married or have children. Oh, I lived in fear of not being ready to meet the Lord, and every time our pastor gave an altar call, I was the first one at the altar, asking God to forgive me of my sins. I didn't want to be caught off-guard and full of sin when the Lord returned!

My grandmother thought she would live to see the second coming of Jesus in the sky. My mother was convinced she would love to be raptured up when the trumpet of the Lord sounded. It was only natural that the little girl I was also believed that I would not die but would be caught up forever to be with the Lord in the sky. But when it didn't happen in Grandma's day, and then it didn't happen for Mom, my hopes grew dim that I would be around for the rapture.

Well, watching television the other night, I began to believe once again that it really *could* happen in my generation. All the Bible prophecies that need to be fulfilled before the Lord can return for His own *have* been fulfilled. They have been fulfilled in my lifetime! You just have to turn on the news to see it for yourself!

Preachers don't preach it anymore . . . at least none that I know of. I feel that there are people that attend church somewhere every Sunday and have never heard a sermon preached on the second coming of the Lord. I'm sure there are young people who have never ever heard that one day "the trumpet of the Lord is going to sound and the dead in Christ shall rise and then we who are living and yet remain shall rise to meet the Lord in the air."

Now I would think that that is something young people could sink their teeth into! It sounds supernatural . . . like flying saucers and UFOs. The kind of stuff TV shows are made of. But the second coming of the Lord or "the rapture of the Church" is not a made-for-TV movie. It's real! It is going to happen! You can read all about it yourself in the Bible.

When I heard those two preachers talking on TV the other night, I was astounded by how long it had been since I actually lived in expectancy of the Lord's imminent return. But as of today, I am once again thinking about and anticipating the coming of the Lord. I want to be ready to go when that trumpet sounds. The Bible says it will happen "in the twinkling of an eye." Two will be sleeping, one will be gone, the other left. Can you imagine a plane filled with people and suddenly the pilot disappears? Imagine driving down the freeway and cars start crashing all around you as the drivers are all suddenly *gone!* The greatest pandemonium that has ever hit this earth will take place at that moment when all of God's people are suddenly gone. Disappeared! Dads and Moms gone; children gone; Grandmas and Grandpas gone! Millions of people, all gone!

If you haven't asked Jesus to come into your heart and forgive you of your sins, *now is the time, my friend!* Don't wait!

It's as simple as a heartfelt prayer:

Dear Jesus, I believe that you are the Son of God, that you were born of the virgin, and that you gave your life on the cross at Calvary because you loved me. I believe that you died for my sins. But you did not stay dead; you rose again and are now sitting at the right hand of your Father, making intercession for me. Forgive me of my sins and come into my heart.

Now Jesus, please give me the strength I need to change the things I need to change in my life and live for you. And when I fall, and I will, help me to ask your forgiveness, pick myself up, dust myself off, and start all over again. I know, Jesus, that you believe in me and that there is nothing I have done that is so bad that you will not forgive me.

I have found that talking to God every day has helped me stay close to Him. Jesus is my best friend. When everyone else turned his or her back on me, I knew that I still had Jesus! And I felt in my heart and soul His peace and His comfort and His unspeakable joy, in spite of the circumstances I was going through at the time. I talk to God in the car, as I work about the house, and as I am shopping. I talk to Him far more than I talk to any of my friends. You see, to me, Jesus is as real as you are. I don't just know about Him in my head, I have Him close to me in my heart. I know that as long as I have a relationship with Jesus, I will never be alone. And I know that whatever happens in my life or to my life is "the will of God in Christ Jesus concerning me." Knowing that God is in control of my life has kept me sane through some terrible situations. Knowing that He has promised not to put more on me than I can bear has kept me strong.

I strongly encourage you to start reading the Bible. If you're not familiar with the Bible, I would suggest you get a Bible called *The Living Bible.* It is more easily understood, as it uses today's language. When you first start reading it, some will find it boring or difficult to understand, but if you just keep at it, reading every day—even if it is just a verse or two at first—you will start to understand it and you will start to *crave* it, just like you crave food. Actually, that is what the Bible is—spiritual food. And we need to feed our souls every day!

Give God a chance, give the Bible a chance. I dare you! If you have tried everything else and there is still something missing in your life, I promise that God will fill that void.

My Favorite Scriptures

Fear thou not for I am with thee, be not dismayed for I am thy God: I will strengthen thee: yea I will help thee; yea I will uphold thee with the right hand of my righteousness.

Isaiah 41:10

My grace is sufficient for thee: for my strength is made perfect in weakness.

2 Corinthians 12:9

For God hath not given us the spirit of fear: but of POWER and of LOVE and of a SOUND MIND.

2 Timothy 1:7

The Lord is my light and my salvation; whom shall I fear? the Lord is the strength of my life; of whom shall I be afraid?

Psalm 27:1

In the day when I cried thou answeredst me, and strengthenedst me with strength in my soul.

Psalm 138:3

Thou wilt keep him in perfect peace, whose mind is stayed on thee: because he trusteth in thee.

Isaiah 26:3 *(continued)*

My Favorite Scriptures *(cont'd)*

He staggered not at the promise of God through unbelief: but was strong in faith, giving glory to God: and being fully persuaded that what He had promised, He was able to perform.

Romans 4:20–21

In everything give thanks: for this is the will of God in Christ Jesus concerning you.

1 Thessalonians 5:18

If we confess our sins, he is faithful and just to forgive us our sins, and to cleanse us from all unrighteousness.

1 John 1:9

I will instruct thee and teach thee in the way which thou shalt go: I will guide thee with mine eye.

Psalm 32:8

And we know that all things work together for good to them that love God, to them that are the called according to his purpose.

Romans 8:28

Call unto me, and I will answer thee, and shew thee great and mighty things, which thou knowest not.

Jeremiah 33:3

But my God shall supply all your need according to His riches in glory by Christ Jesus.

Philippians 4:19

He that dwelleth in the secret place of the most High shall abide under the shadow of the Almighty.

I will say of the Lord, He is my refuge and my fortress: my God: in Him will I trust.

Surely he shall deliver thee from the snare of the fowler, and from the noisome pestilence.

He shall cover thee with his feathers, and under his wings shalt thou trust, his truth shall be thy shield and buckler.

Thou shalt not be afraid for the terror by night nor for the arrow that flieth by day,

Nor for the pestilence that walketh in the darkness nor for the destruction that wasteth at noonday,

A thousand shall fall at thy side, ten thousand at thy right hand, but it shall not come neigh thee,

Only with thine eyes shall thou behold and see the reward of the wicked,

Because thou hast made the Lord which is my refuge, even the most high, thy habitation.

There shall be no evil befall thee, neither shall any plague come nigh thy dwelling.

For he shall give his angels charge over thee, to keep thee in all thy ways.

They shall bear thee up in their hands lest thou dash thy foot against a stone. *(continued)*

My Favorite Scriptures *(cont'd)*

Thou shall tread upon the lion and the adder: the young lion and the dragon shalt thou trample under feet,

Because he hath set his love upon me, therefore will I deliver him: I will set him on high because he hath known my name.

He shall call upon me and I will answer him: I will be with him in trouble;

I will deliver him and honor him.

With long life will I satisfy him and shew him my salvation.

Psalm 91

49.

Your Hut
Is Burning

I have read this countless times on the Internet, and I wish I knew the author. This simple parable just touches my heart and I hope it touches yours too.

The only survivor of a shipwreck was washed up on a small, uninhabited island. He prayed feverishly for God to rescue him, and every day he scanned the horizon for help, but none seemed forthcoming.

Exhausted, he eventually managed to build a little hut out of driftwood to protect himself from the elements and in which to store his few possessions.

But then one day, after scavenging for food, he arrived home to find his little hut in flames, the smoke rolling up to the sky. The worst had happened; everything was lost. He was stunned with grief and anger.

"God, how could you do this to me!" he cried.

Early the next day, however, he was awakened by the sound

of a ship that was approaching the island. It had come to rescue him.

"How did you know I was here?" asked the weary man of his rescuers.

"We saw your smoke signal," they replied.

It is easy to get discouraged when things are going bad. But we shouldn't lose heart, because God is at work in our lives, even in the midst of pain and suffering.

Remember, the next time your little hut is burning to the ground—it just may be a smoke signal that summons the grace of God.

For all the negative things we have to say to ourselves, God has a positive answer for it.

You say: "It's impossible!"
God says: All things are possible (Luke 18:27).

You say: "I'm too tired!"
God says: I will give you rest (Matthew 11:28).

You say: "Nobody really loves me!"
God says: I love you (John 3:16 and John 13:34).

You say: "I can't go on!"
God says: My grace is sufficient (2 Corinthians 12:9 and Psalm 91:15).

You say: "I can't figure things out!"
God says: I will direct your steps (Proverbs 3:5–6).

You say: "I can't do it!"
God says: You can do all things (Philippians 4:13).

You say: "I'm not able!"
God says: I am able (2 Corinthians 9:8).

You say: "It's not worth it!"
God says: It will be worth it (Romans 8:28).

You say: "I can't forgive myself!"
God says: I forgive you (1 John 1:9 and Romans 8:1).

You say: "I can't manage!"
God says: I will supply all your needs (Philippians 4:19).

You say: "I'm afraid!"
God says: I have not given you a spirit of fear (2 Timothy 1:7).

You say: "I'm always worried and frustrated!"
God says: Cast all your cares on me (1 Peter 5:7).

You say: "I don't have enough faith!"
God says: I've given everyone a measure of faith (Romans 12:3).

You say: "I'm not smart enough!"
God says: I give you wisdom (1 Corinthians 1:30).

You say: "I feel all alone!"
God says: I will never leave you or forsake you (Hebrews 13:5).

Pass this on. You never know whose life may be in need of this today. There are some weeks that we all feel our huts are burning.

"I thank my God every time I remember you" (Philippians 1:3).

50.

Final
Thoughts

Two little boys *were given the chore of cleaning out a very dirty barn. It was filled with horse manure.*

One little boy began to cry his heart out. The task seemed insurmountable to his little boy eyes and mind. He pounded on the barn door, begging his dad to let him out.

The other little boy surveyed the messy situation, grabbed a shovel, and began to dig. His words will never be forgotten: "With all this manure, there must be a pony in here somewhere!"

I have shoveled and waded through a lot of manure in my life, but guess what . . . I FOUND THE PONY!

And if you will just be faithful and keep digging, you will too.